Virginia County Records

Volume X

EDITED BY

William Armstrong Crozier

CLEARFIELD

Originally Published As
Virginia County Records
Volume X
The Genealogical Association
Hasbrouck Heights, New Jersey, 1912

Reprinted
Genealogical Publishing Company
Baltimore, 1971

Reprinted for
Clearfield Company by
Genealogical Publishing Co.
Baltimore, Maryland
1993, 1998, 2008

Library of Congress Catalogue Card Number 67-29835
ISBN-13: 978-0-8063-0473-1
ISBN-10: 0-8063-0473-1

Made in the United States of America

The publisher gratefully acknowledges
the loan of the original of this book
by the
Maryland Historical Society
Baltimore, Maryland

Virginia
County Records

EDITED BY

William Armstrong Crozier, F. R. S., F. G. S. A.

The Genealogical Association, Publishers
Hasbrouck Heights
New Jersey

VOLUME X. 1912

College of Arms of Canada

Founded by Edict of King Louis XIV., in 1664. Confirmed by Royal Commission of the Appeal of Malta 1877.

OFFICERS.

The Baron de Longueuil, Chancellor of the Aryan and Seigneurial, Orders.

The Viscount de Fronsac, Herald-Marshal, Huntingdon, P. Q., Canada.

Hon. Thomas Scott Forsyth, Registrar-General, 19 Hanover Street. Montreal, Canada.

COMMISSIONERS.

Henry Black Stuart, Esq., C. E., Sexton Villa, Westmount, Montreal, Canada.

Rev. J. B. Pyke, M. A., 19 Hanover Street. Montreal, Canada.

SOLICITOR-GENERAL IN THE UNITED STATES.

Sir John Calder Gordon, 17 Milk Street, Boston, Mass.

DEPUTY COMMISSIONER IN THE UNITED STATES.

William Armstrong Crozier, Esq., F. R. S., F. G. S. A., Hasbrouck Heights, N. J.

YELLOW ROSE PERSUYVANT.

J. G. B. Bulloch, Esq., M. D., 2122 P. Street, N. W. Washington, D. C.

REPRESENTATIVE IN GREAT BRITAIN.

The Marquis de Ruvigny, 14 Hanover Chambers, Buckingham St., Strand, W. C., London.

REPRESENTATIVE IN FRANCE.

M. Louis Denys de Bonaventure, Chateau d'Aytre, Charente Inferieure

OFFICIAL PUBLICATION.

The Virginia County Records and Heraldic Quarterly Register of the United States and Canada.

CONTENTS OF PART I

Virginia County Records

AND HERALDIC QUARTERLY REGISTER

Vol. X	1912	Part I

INDEX TO LAND GRANTS

RICHMOND COUNTY.

(Continued from Vol. IX.)

Book No. 5.

122	Alexander Scott	1714	450
123	Henry Ashton	1715	2772
125	John Morton, Jr.	1715	200
136	John Corbin	1717	56
140	Capt. Wm. Woodbridge	1717 28A.	28 Per.
151	Alexander Clement	1716	200
153	Mark Harding	1716	122½
154	George Whitley	1717	400
156	Thomas Taylor	1716 408A.	60 Per.
158	Wm. Browne	1717 74A.	58 Per.
160	Patrick Grady	1715	250A.
161	Joseph and George Ball	1717	1085
162	Joseph Chambers	1716	200
165	Charles Morgan	1717	83
171	George Eskridge	1717	2060
175	Metcalfe Dickinson	1718	167
177	Col. Edward Barrow	1717	300
181	Mary Doyle	1717	249
183	Benjamin Strother	1718	50
184	John and Rice Hooe, Jr.	1718	2900
188	George Heal	1718	800
191	Jonas Williams	1718	282
193	Wm. Allen	1718	1490
195	Morgan Griffin	1718	91
197	John Rush	1718	560
198	Wm. Browne	1719	39
203	John Crutcher	1719	358
205	Thomas Bryan	1719	248
206	Capt. George Eskridge	1719	248
215	Lawrence Butler	1719	597
221	Samuel Samford	1719	76
223	Samuel Samford	1719	....
224	Wm. Skrein	1719	833
230	Alexander Beach	1719	606
231	Edmund Jenings	1716	1725
233	Edmund Jenings	1716	850
234	Thomas Simms	1717	112
237	Wm. Walker	1718	100

VIRGINIA COUNTY RECORDS. 3

238 Elias Daviss 1719   49
243 Wm. Phillipps 1719   100
245 John Ferguson 1719   325
144 Nicholas Minor 1715   100
239 Thomas Lee 1718 4200

BOOK "A."

1 John Toon ....1722 86A. 22 Per.
32 Wm. Garland ....1723 101A. 2R. 14 Per.
36 Samuel Algar 1724   40A.
38 Mary Colston ....1724 586A. 144 Per.
148 John Petty ....1725 26A. 152 Pos.
216 Thomas Dale ....1726 126A.
225 Wm. Garland ....1726 499A. 1R. 16 Per.

BOOK "B."

26 Wm. Garland ....1726 128A. 1R. 26 Per.
29 John Carter 1726   600A.
62 Capt. Thomas Beal ....1727 339A. 120P.
63 John Brichley 1727   73A.
64 Gilbert Metcalfe ....1727 843A.
65 Col. John Tayloe 1727   371
67 Wm. Smith ....1727 550A. 63 Per.
68 Humphrey Thomas ....1727 514A. 10 Per.
69 Thomas Williams ....1727 200A.
70 Capt. Moore Fantleroy ....1727 361A. 156 Per.
71 Capt. Moore Fantleroy 1727   81A.
115 Elizabeth Hopwood 1727   150
133 Stephen Lucas 1728   150
137 Thomas Legg 1728   257

BOOK "C."

51 Anthony Sydnor 1729   35
67 Samuel Barber 1730   14

BOOK "E."

3 John Alverson 1736   192
141 John Oldham 1739   401

267 Richard Barnes 1741 90
308 Francis Jackson and Thomas Jordan.....1741 524
461 Edmund Northern 1742 348

Book "F."

210 Daniel Neale 1744 53
255 John Mitchell 1746 70
272 Richard Barnes 1747 210
363 Travers Tarpley ....1754 216A. 2R. 26 Po.
365 Wm. Flood ....1754 153A.

Book "H."

552 Wm. Forrester 1754 226

Book "I."

9 Wm. Barber 1757 243
55 John Hammond 1761 39¼
115 John Tayloe 1764 69
138 James Jervis 1765 47
154 Wm. Northern 1766 312
159 Betty Hill 1767 116
224 Charles Hammond, Jr. 1772 212
259 George Nash ....1774 119A. 1R. 16 Po.
303 Charles Barber ....1777 168A. 1R.
339 Charles Barber ....1778 373A. 18 Po.

ACCOMAC COUNTY.
(Continued from Vol. VII.)

553 Capt. Daniel Junifer 1674-5 1680
607 Edward Robins 1675-6 680
607 Thos. Heady 1675-6 475
608 John Thompson 1675-6 300
609 Wm. Anderson 1676 450
615 Capt. Daniel Jenifer 1677 5800
637 Thos. Wellborne 1678 83
637 Chas. Scarburgh 1678 2100
637 Col. Southey Littleton 1678 1000

638	Major Edmund Bowman 1678	300
638	Richard Holland 1678	600
638	Capt. Chas. Scarburgh and Maj. John West 1678	400
640	Capt. Daniel Jennifer 1678	1680
652	John Cole 1678	650
676	John Washbourne 1679	600
676	Col. Southey Littleton 1678	2800
677	Col. Southey Littleton 1679	150
677	W. Robert Hutchinson 1679	1125
677	Mr. Robert Hutchinson 1679	1125
664	Hancock Lee 1678	268

Book No. 7.

14	Lieut. Col. John West 1679	2500
15	Nathaniel Bradford 1679	644
26	Major General John Custes 1680	100
66	John Tankard 1680	2000
113	Thos. Hunt, John Floyd, Edmund Bibby and George Carke 1681	2200
117	Mr. Wm. Burton 1681	500
123	Capt. John Wallop, alias Wadlow 1682	2350
129	John Custis, Esq. 1682	850
143	Wm. Burton 1682	1000
149	John Wallop, alias Wadlow 1682	1800
157	Wm. Taylor, Jr., and Elias Taylor......1682	200
160	Col. John Custis 1682	3700
173	Wm. Custis, Gent. 1682	1350
182	Col. John Custis 1682	850
185	Col. John Custis 1682	4600
185	Capt. John Wallop, alias Wadlow.......1682	350
195	Benj. Ayres and John Stokeley 1682	175
228	John Barnes & George Parker 1682	350
269	Col. Wm. Stevens & Col. Daniel Jenifer..1683	200
269	Col. Daniel Jenifer 1683	220
295	Benj. Ayres and John Stokeley.........1683	175
395	Thos. Clayton 1684	5800

491	Col. Wm. Kendall	1686	200
493	Adam Mekeels	1686	600
500	Capt. Wm. Custis	1686	800
495	Col. Wm. Kendall	1686	400
524	Mr. John Revell	1686	450
526	Capt. Wm. Whittington	1685	1300
536	Lieut.-Col. Daniel Jenifer	1686	220
537	Lieut.-Col. Daniel Jenifer	1686	170
537	Lieut.-Col. Daniel Jenifer	1686	200
546	Geo. Nicholas Hack	1687	700
589	John Parker of Mattopony	1687	200
563	Col. Daniel Jenifer	1682	3500
563	Isaac Metcalfe	1687	100
577	Thos. Hunt, John Floyd, Edmund Bibbie and George Clark	1687	3350
585	Philip Fisher	1687	150
592	Capt. Wm. Custis	1687	36
615	Maj. Chas. Scarburgh	1687	30
647	George Parker	1688	250
647	Richard Garretson	1688	268
706	Daniel Neeck	1688	200
713	Perry Letherbury	1689	1000

Book No. 8.

30	John Parker	1690	200
32	Thomas, William and Robert Bell	1690	150
40	Thos. Wellbourne	1690	550
64	Col. John West	1690	200
109	Mr. Samuel Taylor	1690	600
110	Mr. Samuel Taylor	1690	300
110	John Morris and John Read	1690	550
129	Col. Daniel Jenifer	1691	200
159	George Truet, Jr., son of Hy. Truet, decd.	1691	100
162	John Morris	1691	300
200	John Willis, Jr.	1691	150
200	John Willis, Jr.	1691	250
235	Wm. Kendall	1692	2725
236	John Wallop, alias Wadlow	1692	2500

 72 Elizabeth Scarburgh, widow, and Anthony
         West 1713   900
 73 Arthur Upshur 1713   2300
137 Wm. and Nathaniel Bell 1714   90
181 Jonathan West 1714   50
185 Mrs. Matilda West 1714   2730
213 John Bonwell 1714   400
232 Francis Eyers 1714   579
287 Chas. Bailey and John Sparrow 1715   450
327 Thos. Gascoine 1717   1093
332 Philip Parker and Chas. Parker 1717   50

Book No. 11.

233 Wm. Custis, Gent. 1723   1013

Book No. 12.

379 Arthur Robins 1726   1907

Book No. 13.

111 John Marshall 1727   170

Book No. 14.

 36 Henry Satchell 1730   40
318 George Parker 1731   496

Book No. 22.

598 George Douglas 1745   100

Book No. 24.

537 Richard Drummond 1746   250
153 Wm. Gibb 1746   20

Book No. 25.

255 Edmond Scarburgh, Jr. 1746   200

Book No. 26.

708 Ambrose Benson 1748   132

Book No. 27.

 97 Peter Marshall 1748   150

Book No. 32.

Book No. 33.

Book No. 35.

Book No. 37.

Book No. 42.

Book No. 11.

Book No. 25.

Book No. 31.

Book No. 32.

CHESTERFIELD COUNTY WILLS.

(By W. G. Stanard.)

Will of Joseph Mayo of Henrico (no date and no probate).
Legatees, wife, Frances; unborn child, daughter Frances
Moseley. William Moseley, Sr., executor.
West 1713   170

Will of Matthew Moseley, dated November 9, 1768 (the inventory of his estate recorded 1769). Legatees, wife, son Blackman Moseley, each of his children; mentions land where testator's father then lived; son William, son Joseph (including land testator bought of his (the testator's) brother Joseph), daughters Frances and Martha, wife Martha. Wife and John Archer, Jr., executors.

Account October 7, 1772, February, 1773, with the estate of William Moseley, deceased, and inventory filed by Joseph Moseley, executor. He refers to "My father's bond," so Joseph Moseley was probably son of William.

Will of William Moseley, date July 10, 1778. Legatees daughter, Sarah Marshall; grandmother, Sarah Marshall; granddaughter, Sarah Moseley; granddaughter, Frances Moseley, daughter of son William; grandson, Matthew Moseley; grandson, Thomas Moseley; grandson, John Moseley; to son Matthew's four children the four negroes son Matthews had the use of, to go according to said Matthew's will; great-grandchild, Matthew, son of Blackman Moseley; daughter-in-law, Mary, widow of William Moseley; granddaughter, Elizabeth Featherstone, son Matthew's three sons. Grandson, Blackman Moseley, and William Walthall, Jr., executors.

Will of Matthew Moseley, dated March 7, 1789 (probably proved in same year), gives all estate to cousin, Blackman Moseley, and makes him executor, "he being in low circumstances in the world (i. e., poor)."

Will of Thomas Moseley, dated March 4, 1780. Legatees, mother to have whole estate while she lives, and at her death to be divided between his sisters, Sarah and Frances Moseley. Blackman Moseley, executor.

Will of Drury Ragsdale, dated November 17, 1749 (inventory recorded June 24, 1750). Legatees, wife Margaret, unborn child; brother, Joseph Ragsdale. His Lunenburg land to be sold. (To his family belonged Drury Ragsdale, of Virginia, who was a captain in the First Continental Artillery in the Revolutionary War.)

Will of Littlebury Royall, dated July 10, 1749. Legatees, sons Joseph, Littlebury and John, wife Mary. Wife and brothers, Richard and John Royall, executors.

Will of Caleb Ware, dated June 28, 1740, proved March 22, 1749. (This will had been disputed). Legatees, Matthew Branch, Sr., John Branch, Sr., Mary, wife of James Branch; Mary, wife of William Puckett, deceased; Matthew Branch, Jr.

Will of William Gay, dated March 1, 1749, to wife Elizabeth, all lands in Chesterfield and Cumberland counties, and all rest of estate. (Dr. William Gay married Elizabeth, daughter of Major John Bolling, of "Cobbs." For descendants, see Robertson's "Pocahontas and Her Descendants.")

Will of Elizabeth Cary, dated May 31, 1750. Legatees, Mrs. Judith Bell, £100 current money and my gold watch, chain and seal; Mrs. Sarah Spiers, £100; Ann, daughter of Archibald Cary, £100 current money; Henry Bell £500 current money, to be laid out in land and negroes; John Brickenhead, peruke maker, in Old Street, near St. Luke's Church, London, £200; goddaughter, Betty Cary, £20; Rev. Mr. Fraser, my waiting man James; godson, George Fraser, £20. (This was the widow of Henry Cary, of "Ampthill," Chesterfield county, and the mother of Archibald Cary of Revolutionary fame, who on his mother's death, removed from Cumberland county to "Ampthill." Henry and Elizabeth Cary also had two daughters—Judith, who married David Bell, of Buckingham county, and Sarah, who married ———— Spiers, a Scotchman.)

Will of Henry Cary, dated May 27, 1748. By a marriage contract with his wife, Elizabeth, he agreed to leave her £1,000 in money, and he therefore bequeaths her that amount in sterling, and also £220 current money in consideration of the like amount he had received from the sale of her house in Williamsburg. He also bequeaths to her for her life all the household goods and plate he

had received with her, and at her death to son Archibald;
also to wife, Elizabeth, a negro man named James he had
received with her. In consideration of a marriage between his daughter, Judith, and David Bell, he had put
said Bell in possession of 3,000 acres on Hatcher's Creek,
in Albemarle (now in Buckingham), part of a larger
tract, with thirteen negroes, and all cattle, utensils, etc.,
on said land, he now confirms said gift; but if he (the
testator) should die before his wife they are to lay off
1,000 for the use of his (the testator's) wife and daughter, Judith Bell, during their lives, and the said slaves to
be for the same purpose, and after the death of David
Bell and Judith, his wife, said land and slaves are to
descend to testator's grandson, Henry Bell. To grandson, Henry Bell, a negro; to son-in-law, Alexander
Spiers, 3,000 acres of land, near Willis's Creek, now in
possession of said Spiers, and all stocks, etc., on said land,
and also two negroes; all rest of estate to son Archibald.

Will of Jeremiah Walthall, dated February 8, 1747-8.
Legatees, Mary Bass, friend Joseph Farley's son, Forrest
Farley; brothers William and John Walthall; brother
William's son, William, and daughter, Mary, brother
Henry's sons, Thomas and Henry, and his daughter,
Anne. To brother Henry's son the land testator lives on
and other land to Henry's son, Jeremiah. Brother Henry
Walthall, executor.

Will of William Worsham, dated December 19, 1752.
Legatees, wife Annie, bequest to educate daughter, Elizabeth Eppes (Worsham). Father-in-law, Isham Eppes,
executor.

Will of Joseph Ligon, dated November 17, 1751. Legatees,
son Joseph, part of the land testator lived on called Rock-
dale; son John, son Thomas, two tracts in Amelia, 800
and and 469 acres; son William, 612 acres on Sandy
River, Amelia; William Baugh, Jr., 160 acres called
Boldens; daughter, Mary Moseley, one negro; now in
possession of testator's father; daughters Martha, Eliza-

beth and Judith Ligon; wife, as Prince Edward county was formed from Amelia after 1751, no doubt Thomas Watkins Ligon, Governor of Maryland 1854-1858, who was a native of Prince Edward, was of this family.)

Will of William Baugh, dated January 12, 1753. Legatees, sons John, Frederick and William; daughter, Agnes Baugh; daughter, Sarah Walthall; sister, Sarah Stuart.

Will of John Worsham, dated December 8, 1751. Legatees, son Joshua; daughter, Phoeby Jones; son Thomas, grandson John and John Worsham. Inventory of John Worsham, deceased, recorded October 5, 1753.

Inventory of William Worsham, Jr., deceased, recorded 1753.

Inventory of Godfrey Ragsdale, deceased, recorded June 6, 1755.

Inventory of Richard Walthall, deceased, recorded about 1755.

Will of Thomas Cary, dated August 12, 1754 (inventory dated October, 1755.) Legatees, son Robert, land on Pokoshock; son Thomas, wife Dorothy.

Will of Magdalen Salle, dated August 3, 1756, all estate to daughter, Elizabeth Salle.

Will of William Robertson, dated April 4, 1757. Legatees, wife Frances, sons James and William, grandson, John Robertson, son of William, daughters, Margaret Rudd, Frances Baugh and Mary Owen; son-in-law, John Claiborne; daughter, Jennett.

Inventory of William Robertson, deceased, recorded October 23, 1758.

Will of Essex Worsham, dated November 8, 1758. Legatees, sons Drury, Henry and William, wife Anne, daughter, Phoebe Harper.

Will of John Osborne, dated March 27, 1760. Legatees, wife Ann, mention of land where the public warehouses stand; sons, John and Thomas; daughters Frances, Martha and Ann; states that he has been at great expense building on the land adjoining the warehouses, and empowers friend, Thomas Friend, Jr., and brother, Francis Osborne, to make sale of the residue of the lands adjoining.

(John Osborne owned the land on James River on which the little town of Osbornes was laid out. It was almost entirely destroyed by British troops during the Revolutionary; but "Osbornes" was long the shipping point for the Clover Hill coal mines.)

Will of James Deans, merchant, dated April 20, 1764. Legatees, to wife Caroline, £1,500 current money, all household furniture, stocks of horses, cattle, etc., his chair and horses, all negroes except two women who are devised to daughter Mary; to sisters, Katherine and Christian Deans, an annuity of £30; rest of estate to daughter Mary; and if she dies then £200 to Ann and Margaret, daughters of friend James Murray, and £200 to the infirmary of Aberdeen, Scotland, and rest of estate to wife; £30 annually for board and education of daughter. Friends Richard Bland, of Jordans; James Murray, of Athole Braes, Prince George, and William Fleming, of Cumberland, executors.

Will of Thomas Bott, dated August 6, 1776. Legatees: Grandson, William Bell (including a negro which said William's mother, Ann Bell, had of William Bott); granddaughter, Mary, wife of John Wilson; daughter, Ann, wife of William Hall; son, Miles Bott; son, William Bott; wife, Ann; son, John Bott.

Will of Peter Baugh, dated October 16, 1773. Legatees: Son, Peter; daughter, Jane Stratton; daughter, Elizabeth Hill; daughter, Frances De Leau; daughter, Sarah Smith; daughter, Ann Folkes; sons, Robert, James and Burwell Baugh; wife, Elizabeth.

Will of Betty Todd, dated October 30, 1777. Legatees: Granddaughter, Betty Todd; son, Thomas Todd; daughter, Milly Todd; son, Richard Todd; William Dandridge, of Henrico, and Dr. William McKenzie, of Chesterfield, executors.

Will of Thomas Walthall, dated December 12, 1776. Legatees: Eldest son, Henry, wife; son, More Walthall; daughter, Elizabeth, "children" (whom he does not name.)

Will of John Markham, dated October 20, 1770. Legatees:
Daughter, Rebecca; daughter, Judith; sons, John, Vincent,
George and Archibald; daughter, Catherine Smith; sons,
William and Bernard.

Will of James Patteson (not Patterson), dated February 23,
1767 (inventory May, 1767). Legatees: Son, Nelson,
lands on Appomattox, and on James River in Amherst
(which testator purchased of David Patteson); daughter,
Sarah Patteson; wife, Mary (probably second wife), wife,
Mary; Thomas Prosser and Charles, son of David Patteson, executors.

Will of William Pride, dated October 4, 1749. Legatees: Son,
John (land in Amelia); son Peter (land testator lives on);
all negroes to be divided between wife and three children.

Will of John Folkes, Sr., dated December 1, 1773. Legatees:
Grandson, John Folkes, after said John's father's and
mother's deaths, the land his (the grandson's) father lives
on, etc.; son, Joel Folkes, grandson, Abel Folkes, all testator's land in Prince Edward, where testator's son, Daniel,
now lives; daughter, Michel Folkes; daughter, Mary
Folkes; sons, Josiah and Francis Folkes; daughter, Amy
Rudd; daughter Edy Claiborne.

Will of Frances Friend, dated June 13, 1772. Legatees:
Daughter, Judith Friend; sons, Edward, Joseph and Nathaniel; daughters Ann and Frances Osborne.

Will of John Hylton, dated November 7, 1773. Legatees:
Wife, all his land at Bermuda Hundred and that called
Lower Liggons, in Chesterfield, for her life, and at her
death to his youngest son, Bowler; son, John, land called
Baldams; son, Ralph, lands in Bedford, lands in Charles
City to be sold; to each daughter a slave; wife and
daughters, Elizabeth and Sarah Cocke (Hilton?) £500 cur-
rent money each. Charles Carter, Esq., of Corotoman;
Francis Eppes, of Wintopock; John Archer, Thomas
Jefferson, wife and son, John Hylton, executors.

Will of Edward Ligon, dated January 13, 1775. Legatees:
Sons, Thomas, Edward, and William; daughters, Mary

Lockett, Elizabeth Christian (or Chastain), Edith, Sarah
and Milly Ligwood; son, Archibald. Executors to pay for
education of son, William, this year.

Will of John Ligon, dated December 26, 1773 (inventory September, 1774). Legatees: Wife, Mary, land in Prince
Edward; to mother, Judith Ligon, an annuity from lands
in Cumberland; daughter, Mary Ligon; children, John,
Thomas and Mary.

Will of Henry Walthall, dated May 28, 1766. Legatees: Son,
Henry; son, Archibald, land in Chesterfield and Prince
Edward; daughter, Molly; son, William, daughter, Ann
Branch; wife, Ann.

Will of Martha Walthall, dated May 19, 1771. Legatees:
Daughter, Jane; son, James; daughter, Martha; sons,
Francis and Thomas; daughter, Ann Farmer; grandson,
Benjamin, son of Benjamin Walthall.

Will of John Worsham, Jr., dated November 25, 1768. Legatees: Wife, lots in Bermuda Hundred; brother, Edward Worsham; sister, Mary Wilkinson.

HENRICO COUNTY RECORDS.

1 June, 1789. Conveyance from Robert Woodson, Snr.,
County Henrico, to daughter, Sarah, wife of Edward
Moseby, of same place, and their son, John Moseby, when
21 years old, 100 acres of land.

Richard Newcomb, administrator of Thomas Newcomb, who
married the admx. of John Clyborn, decd., records inventory, 21 March, 1688.

Inventory of Thomas Harrison, decd., by Sarah Turpin, 1
June, 1689.

Power of attorney from Judith Field to loving son, Mr. Henry
Randolph, to sell land my husband, Peter Field, had from
James Frankling. 1 August, 1689.

Account of Thomas Bottomlys estate entered by Thomas Osborne, Snr. 1 August, 1689.

Will of Repps Jones, planter, 19 February, 1688; prob. 1

August, 1689. To Philip Turpin and his wife land I bought from my brother, Thomas Jones, and after the decease of said Turpin and wife to my cousin Thomas Jones, and failing heirs then to Edward Skern. My sister, Mary Skern; my sister Martha Osborne; rest of my estate to my mother.

Will of William Ligon, 21 January, 1688; prob. 1 August, 1689. Plantation to be divided between my sons Thomas and William; to son, John; my son, Joseph, and Thomas Farrar, Jnr.; my daughter, Mary, and the child my wife now goes with.

Will of Thomas Jones, 22 January, 1688; prob. 20 August, 1689. My son, Thomas; daughter, Lucretia, when 16 years; wife, Martha Jones.

Conveyance from Thomas Broadway to Moses Wood; Elizabeth, wife of Thomas, releases dower rights. 1 October, 1689.

Conveyance from James Lisle to son, James Lisle, Jnr. 1 October, 1689.

Conveyance from Mary Porter to William Porter. 6 July, 1689.

Conveyance from William Porter to George, son of my brother, John Porter, decd. 1 October, 1689.

Deed of gift from Thomas Cocke to his two granddaughters, Mary and Anne Aust. 1 October, 1689.

Indenture between Robert Cate and Peter Wyke. 7 September, 1689.

Account of estate of Thomas Perrin, decd., by Ann, the widow and admx. 1 October, 1689.

Conveyance from Lionel Morris, of New Kent, and Elizabeth, his wife, of New Kent, to Daniel Price, of Henrico. 2 December, 1689.

Inventory of estate of John Davis, decd. 15 November, 1689.

Account of the cattle belonging to the widow and orphans of Mathew Turpin, decd., children, Henry, Cicely and Mathew Turpin. Presented by Joseph Tanner, who married the widow of Mathew Turpin, decd. 2 December, 1689.

Division of the personal estate of John Lewis, decd., divided
   into three parts; to the relict of John Lewis, now the wife
   of Samuel Trottman, to William Lewis, the son, and to
   Sarah, the daughter. 2 December, 1689.

Will of William Elam, 18 February, 1688; prob. 1 February,
   1689. To son-in-law, John Cox, Jnr., and to cousin,
   Martin Elam.

Inventory of the estate of Richard Tarvin. 28 January, 1689.

Inventory of the estate of Thomas Bottomley returned by
   William Glover, 28 January, 1689.

Conveyance from Samuel Bridgewater, carpenter, to three
   sons, Samuel, Benjamin and Thomas, and two daughters,
   Mary and Elizabeth Bridgewater. 2 December, 1689.

Will of John Burton, 12 February, 1689; 1 April, 1690. To
   son, Robert; to son, William; to daughter, Rachel; to
   granddaughter, Mary Davis; grandson, William Davis;
   granddaughter, Elizabeth Davis, 300 pounds of tobacco
   owed me by John Davis; my daughter, Mary Glover, and
   her daughter, Elizabeth; to Mr. William Glover all my
   corn.

Bond of John Porter, who married the admx. of John Davis,
   decd., to deliver to Francis, son of said Davis, when 16
   years, certain personal property. 1 April, 1690.

Account of Barth. Burrows, decd., estate presented by Robert
   Green, who married the relict. 27 October, 1688.

Escheat granted to Thomas Batte and Amy, his wife, and
   Thomas Batte, Snr., of 400 acres in Henrico, now as-
   signed by said Thomas Batte to John Bevill. 29 February,
   1689.

Deposition of Frances, wife of Samuel Bridgewater. 2 June,
   1690.

Power of attorney from Judith Woodson to cousin, John
   Woodson, Jnr., relinquishing my right of dower in 300
   acres of land sold by my husband, John Woodson, to
   Samuel Knibb and Jeremiah Brown. 2 June, 1690.

Deed of gift from John Woodson, wheelright, to brother,
   Robert Woodson, Jnr., of one-fifth part of a patent

granted to Robert Woodson, Snr., John Woodson and others. 2 June, 1690.

Account of the estate of John Whiteman, decd. 29 March, 1689.

Deed of gift from Thomas East, Snr., to son, Thomas, and daughter, Marvell East. 1 August, 1690.

Deed of gift from Peter Field to two daughters, Mary and Martha Field. 30 April, 1690.

Thomas Batte by order of Court delivered to Essex Bevill 2 cows, and likewise to Mary Bevill, and at the same time Mrs. Amy Batte in behalf of her daughter, Mary Bevill, and ye said Essex Bevill, did acknowledge receipt of same. 20 August, 1690.

Conveyance from Benjamin Hatcher to John Woodson, Snr. Elizabeth, wife of said Benjamin, relinquishes her dower. 31 September, 1690.

Conveyance from Francis Rowen, planter, to Thomas East; Jane, the wife of said Francis, relinquishes her dower, and Alice Watson, mother of said Francis Rowen, having dower rights also relinquishes. 1 December, 1690.

Conveyance from Edward Stratton to Arthur Moseley. Martha, wife of said Edward, and Martha, the relict of Edward Stratton, Snr., decd., also relinquishes her dower. 2 February, 1690.

Will of Jeremiah Brown, 29 November, 1690; prob. 2 February, 1690. My wife, Elizabeth; my beloved mother, Sarah Woodson, to have the land in her possession; to Solomon, second son of Samuel Knibb, of Henrico, when he is 17; to sister, Temperance Batte; to Samuel and John, sons of Samuel Knibb.

Deed of gift from John Price and his wife, Jane, to their daughter, Mary Price. 2 February, 1690.

Inventory of the estate of Nathaniel Hill, decd. 16 February, 1690.

Inventory of estate of William Harris, decd., by George Archer, the adm. 28 May, 1690.

Indenture made 25 April, 1691, between John Gundry, of the county of Gloucester, son of John Gundry and Annie, his wife; one of the daughters of Robert Hallam, late of the county of Henrico, decd.; to Captain William Randolph. Mentions Samuel Woodward and Sarah, his wife, younger sister to said Anne Gundry, and their brother ——— Hallam, decd.

Mr. William Farra, sworn High Sheriff of Henrico for the ensuing year of .1691. 1 June, 1691.

Account of the estate of Edward Lucas, decd. 11 June, 1691.

Account of the estate of John Johnson, decd. 18 June, 1691.

EARLY IMMIGRANTS TO VIRGINIA.

(Continued from Vol. IX.)

Hayes, John, transported by William Montague, Middlesex, 7 November, 1700.

Heyley, Eleanor, wife of Rev. Willis Heyley, Mulberry Islands, 8 December, 1635.

Heyley, Robert, brother of Rev. Willis Heyley, Mulberry Island, 8 December, 1635.

Heyward, Humphrey, transported in the "John & Dorothy," 1634, by Capt. Adam Thorogood.

Heywood, John, transported by Thomas Harwood, 7 July, 1635.

Hill, John, transported in the "John & Dorothy," 1634, by Capt. Adam Thorogood.

Hill, Mary, transported in the "John & Dorothy," 1634, by Capt. Adam Thorogood.

Hill, Mary, Jnr., transported by Capt. Adam Thorogood, 24 June, 1635.

Hinckley, Thomas, transported by Thomas Harwood, 7 July 1635.

Hunton, Robert, transported by John Pate and Robert Beverley, 15 July, 1669. Hickmore, Sarah (servant), transported by Capt. Francis Epes, 26 August, 1635.

Hinds, William, transported in the "Friendship," 1629, by Capt. Adam Thorogood.

Hitchcock, Richard, transported by William Barker, 26 November, 1635.

Holland, Henry, servant, transported by William Stone, Accomac, 4 June, 1635.

Holley, Mournful, transported in the "Africa," by Capt. Adam Thorogood, 24 June, 1635.

Hollier, Julina, transported in the "Katherine," in 1623, by John Moone.

Holloway, Peter, transported by Hugh Cox, 6 December, 1634.

Holmes, John, transported in the "Southampton," in 1623, by William Ferrar, Esq.

Home, John, transported by James Knott, Elizabeth City, 20 March, 1635.

Hudson, Henry, transported by William Montague, Middlesex, 7 November, 1700.

Holt, Randolph (servant), transported by John Pott, James City, 1632.

Holton, John, transported in "John & Dorothy," 1634, by Capt. Adam Thorogood.

Holton, William, transported in the "John & Dorothy," 1634, by Capt. Adam Thorogood.

Honyborne, Robert (servant), transported by Edward Sparshott, Charles City, 20 November, 1635.

Hooper, Thomas, transported by William Barker, 26 November, 1635.

Hopkins, Phoebus (servant), transported by George Sandys, of Archers Hope, in 1721.

Hopkins, Robert, transported by John Sparkes, 3 June, 1635.

Hound, Darius, transported by John Brewer, 11 June, 1635.

Howe, John, transported by William Ravanett, of County of Denbeigh, 21 November, 1635.

Howell, Cob, transported in the "John & Dorothy," 1634, by Capt. Adam Thorogood.

Howell, Owen, transported by John Upton, 7 July, 1735.

Howell, Walter, transported by Capt. Thomas Willoughby, 19 March, 1634.

Howes, John, transported in the "Neptune," in 1618, by Lieut. Golbert Peppet.

Hudson, Elizabeth, transported by Henry Daniell, of James City, 13 November, 1635.

Hudson, Robert, transported by Thomas Harwood, 7 July, 1635.

Huett, Morgan, transported by Robert Cane, 18 December, 1635.

Huitt, John, transported in the "Hopewell," in 1633, by Capt. Adam Thorogood.

Hull, Jeffrey (servant), transported in the " George," in 1611, by Elizabeth Clements.

Hunt, John, transported by William Woolritch, of Elizabeth City, 17 June, 1635.

Jackson, Richard, transported by Capt. Thomas Willoughby, 6 November, 1635.

Jackson, Thomas, transported by George Keith, 29 July, 1635.

Jackson, William, transported by William Barker, 26 November, 1635.

Jacob, Andrew, transported by William Swan, of James City, 5 November, 1635.

James, Hugh (servant), transported by Capt. Francis Epes, 26 August, 1635.

James, John, transported by Capt. Adam Thorogood, 18 December, 1835.

Jego, Richard, transported by Capt. Adam Thorogood, 24 June, 1635.

Johnson, Joyce, transported by Capt. Adam Thorogood, 18 December, 1635.

Johnson, Elizabeth, headright, wife of Joseph Johnson, 19 June, 1635.

Johnson, Henry, and Grace, his wife, transported by Richard Bennett, 26 June, 1635.

Johnson, Henry (servant), transported by William Stone, of Accomac, 4 June, 1635.

VIRGINIA COUNTY RECORDS. 23

Johnson, Mary, transported by John Upton, 7 July, 1635.

Johnson, Richard, transported in the "Hopewell," in 1628, by Capt. Adam Thorogood.

Johnson, Robert, transported by William Andrews, of Accomac, 25 June, 1635.

Johnson, Thomas, transported by Capt. William Peirce, 22 June, 1635.

Johnson, Thomas, transported by Capt. Adam Thorogood, 24 June,. 1635.

Johnson, Thomas, transported by William Barker, 26 November, 1635.

James, Howell, transported by Thomas Eyre, of Accomac, 7 November, 1700.

Jones, Edward, transported in the "Friendship," in 1629, by Capt. Adam Thorogood.

Jones, Elias, transported by George Keith, 29 July, 1635.

Jones, Evan (servant), transported by Charles Harmar, 4 July, 1635.

Jones, John, transported by William Barker, 26 November, 1635.

Jones, Hugh, transported by William Wilkinson, minister, 20 November, 1635.

Jones, Rice, of Warwick River, came from Canada at own transportation in the "John & Francis," in 1623.

Jones, Richard, transported by William Swan, of James City, 5 November, 1635.

Jones, Richard, transported by Francis Fowler, of James City County, 1635.

Jones, Richard, transported by John Upton, 7 July, 1635.

Jones, Timothy (servant), transported by William Gany, Accomac, 17 September, 1635.

Jones, Thomas, transported by Jenkins Osborne, 9 July, 1635.

Jones, Thomas, transported by Henry Coleman, 6 June, 1635.

Jones, Thomas, transported by David Jones, 5 July, 1635.

Jones, Thomas, transported by Christopher Woodward, —— 1635.

Jordan, Anthony, transported by John Moone, 21 October, 1635.

24   VIRGINIA COUNTY RECORDS.

Jordan, John, transported by John Brewer, 11 June, 1635.
Jordan, Nicholas, servant, transported by William Gany, Accomac, 17 September, 1635.

(Continued.)

VIRGINIA REVOLUTIONARY SOLDIERS.

Claiborne, Rich., Lieut., Contl. Line, end of war.
Aspinwall, Jno., Private, Contl Line, end of war.
Whiting, Hy., Captain, Contl. Line, 3 years' service.
Noel, Archilles, Sergeant, Contl. Line, 3 years' service.
Haldrop, Thos., Private, Contl. Line, 3 years' service.
Irving, Wm., Sergeant, Contl. Line, 3 years' service.
Treade, Wm., Private, State Line, 3 years' service.
Flin, Thos., Private, Contl. Line, 3 years' service.
Burton, Wm., Private, Sontl. Line, 3 years' service.
Humphries, Jno., Private, Contl. Line, 3 years' service.
Baughan, Wm., Private, Contl. Line, 3 years' service.
Ryland, Jno., Corporal, Contl. Line, 3 years' service.
Clark, Edmond, Lieut., Contl. Line, 3 years' service.
Harrison, Chas., Colonel, Contl. Line, 3 years' service.
Wooten, Thos., Private, Contl. Line, 3 years' service.
Lear, John, Private, Contl. Line, 3 years' service.
Scott, Drury, Private, Contl. Line, 3 years' service.
Welch, Polk, Sergeant, Contl. Line, 3 years' service.
Hall, Jno., Sergeant, Contl. Line, 8 years' service.
Egleston, Wm., Lieut., Contl. Line, 3 years' service. Richd.
    Egleston, representative, 2 February, 1784.
Anderson, Jno., Captain, Contl. Line, 7 years' service.
Monroe, Jas., Major, Contl. Line, 3 years' service.
Hazlewood, Richd., Private, Contl. Line, 3 years' service.
Trent, Thos., Sergeant, Contl. Line, 3 years' service.
Lewis, Zach, Sergeant, Contl. Line, 3 years' service.
Cockran, Saml., Sergeant, Contl. Line, 3 years' service.
Holland, Geo., Lieut., Contl. Line, 3 years' service.
Armistead, Wm., Captain, State Line, 3 years' service.

Walker, Levin, Lieut., State Line, 3 years' service.

Trezevant, John D., Surgeon, Contl. Line, end of war.

Bruce, Geo., Corporal, Contl. Line, 3 years service.

Butler, Saml. Lieut., State Line, end of war.

Marshall, Jas. Markham, Lieut., State Line, end of war.

Quarles, Robt., Lieut., Contl. Line, end of war.

Cockrel, Presley, Private, Contl. Line, 3 years' service.

Perkins, Archelaus, Lieut., Contl. Line, end of war.

Haldrop, Thos., Fifer, Contl. Line, 3 years' service.

Lyne, Barnabus, Private, Contl. Line, 3 years' service.

Dell, Joseph, Private, Contl. Line, 3 years' service.

Woodson, Absolom, Private, Contl. Line, 3 years' service.

Kelly, Andrew, Corporal, Contl. Line, 3 years' service.

Allen, Francis, Corporal, Contl. Line, 3 years' service.

Vasser, Isham, Corporal, Contl. Line, 3 years' service.

Davenport, Joel, Private, Contl. Line, 3 years' service.

Lumt, Joseph, Private, Contl. Line, 3 years' service.

McNeal, David, Private, Contl. Line, 3 years' service.

Briant, Wm., Private, Contl. Line, 3 years' service.

Cheronings, Thos., Private, Contl. Line, 3 years' service.

Toney, Vincent, Private, Contl. Line, 3 years' service.

Fowler, Anderson, Private, Contl. Line, 3 years' service.

Newman, Thos., Private, Contl. Line, 3 years' service.

Tuggle, Hy., Private, Contl. Line, 3 years' service.

Blys, Wm., Private, Contl. Line, 3 years service.

Willoughby, Wm., Private, Contl. Line, 3 years' service.

Harris, Jordan, Lieut., Contl. Line, end of war.

Nichols, Jno., Private, Contl. Line, end of war.

Weaver, Jno., Private, Contl. Line, end of war.

Williams, Jno., Private, Contl. Line, 3 years' service.

Emerson, Hy., Sergeant, Contl. Line, 3 years' service.

Turner, Jno., Lieut., State Line, end of war.

Jones, Jno., Private, Contl. Line., end of war.

Shepherd, Jas., Sergeant, State Line, 3 years' service.

Cluverins, Jas., Captain-Lieut., State Line, 3 years' service.
    Benj. Cluverins, representative, 5 February, 1784.

Linton, Jno., Lieut., Contl. Line, 7 years' service.

Graves, Francis, Private, Contl. Line, 3 years' service.

Stephens, Rich., Private, State Line, 3 years' service.

Richardson, Robert, Private, State Line, 3 years' service.

Devenport, Opie, Lieut., State Line, end of war.

Davison, Josiah, Private, Contl. Line, 3 years' service.

Temple, Benj., Lieut. Colonel, Contl. Line, 3 years' service.

Sears, Thos., Lieut., Contl. Line, end of war.

Carter, Robt., Private, Contl. Line, 3 years' service.

Ellis, Jas., Drummer, State Line, 3 years' service.

Cardwell, Jno., Private, Contl. Line, 3 years' service.

Taylor, Jas., Sergeant, State Line, 3 years' service.

Savoy, Jno., Private, Contl. Line (orig. voucher says State Line), end of war.

Pettus, John, Captain, Contl. Line, 3 years' service. Stephen Pettus, representative, 7 February, 1784.

Nickins, Edw., Sailor, State Navy, 3 years' service.

Hinton, Wm., Sailor, State Navy, 3 years' service.

Wilder, Jas., Sailor, State Navy, 3 years' service.

Fleetwood, Isaac, Sailor, State Navy, 3 years' service.

Allen, Thos., Boatswain, State Navy, 3 years' service.

Cornelius, Wm., Gunner, State Navy, 3 years' service.

Starke, Wm., Lieut., Contl. Line, 3 years' service. Lewis Starke, assignee, 9 February, 1784.

Wollard, Jno., Private, State Line, 3 years' service.

Coleman, Wyatt, Lieut., State Line, 7 years' service.

Brandam, Lewis, Sergeant, Contl. Line, 3 years' service.

Forrest, Zach, Sergeant, Contl. Line, 3 years' service.

Lyon, Wm., Private, Contl. Line, 3 years' service (orig. voucher says State Line).

Thompson, Royal, Private, Contl. Line, 3 years' service.

Mash, Thos., Private, Contl. Line, 3 years' service.

Arnold, Wm., Corporal, Contl. Line, 3 years' service.

Needham, Isaac, Private, Contl. Line, end of war.

Pierce, Wm., Captain, Contl. Line, 7 years' service.

Scott, Chas., Cornet, Contl. Line, end of war.

Barton, Jas., Private, Contl. Line, 3 years' service.

Shelton, Clough, Captain, Contl. Line, 7 years' service.

Bailey, Wm., Private, decd., Contl. Line, 3 years' service. Hy.
   Ba. .ey, representative, —— February, 1784.
Richardson, Wm., Private, State Line, 3 years' service.
Meed, Jno., Sergeant, Contl. Line, end of war.
Evans, Geo., Surgeon, Contl. Line, 3 years' service.
Spencer, Wm., Lieut., State Line, end of war.
Davies, Wm., Colonel, Contl. Line, 3 years' service.
Barbee, Elijah, Private, Contl. Line, end of war.
Wright, Paul, Private, Contl. Line, 3 years' service.
Woosley, Moses, Private, Contl. Line, 3 years' service.
Hancock, Bennett, Private, Contl. Line, end of war.
Aldridge, Rich., Private, Contl. Line, 3 years' service.
Day, Jno., Private, Contl. Line, end of war.
Hill, Gidern, Private, Contl. ᴜine, 3 years' service.
Lenwick, Saml., Corporal, Contl. Line, 3 years' service.
Gregory, Obadiah, Sergeant, Contl. Line, 3 years' service.
Bowers, Jacob, Private, Contl. Line, 3 years' service.
Ridsey, Alex, Private, Contl. Line, 3 years' service.
Mumgrower, Nich., Private, Contl. Line, 3 years' service.
Miller, Robt., Private, Contl. Line, 3 years' service.
Mason, Danl., Private, Contl. Line, 3 years' service.
Jessey, Turner, Sergeant, Contl. Line, 3 years' service.
Merrither, Jas., Lieut., State Line, 3 years' service.
Oakley, Geo., Sergeant, State Line, 3 years' service.
White, Thos., Private, State Line, 3 years' service.
Roach, Jno., Corporal, Contl. Line, 3 years' service.
Rankins, Benj., Private, Contl. Line, 3 years' service.
Elmore, Jno., Sergeant, Contl. Line, 3 years' service.
Hopper, Jno., Private, Contl. Line, 3 years' service.
Higgins, John, Private, State Line, 3 years' service.
Leech, Geo., Private, State Line, 3 years' service.
Kebble, Wm., Corporal, State Line, 3 years' service.
Ragan, Danl., Sergeant, State Line, 3 years' service.
Maynard, Nath., Corporal, State Line, 3 years' service.
Martin, Jno., Sergeant, Contl. Line, 3 years' service.
Thompson, Geo., Lieut., State Line, 3 years' war, to Lucy
   Thompson, wife, Geo. Thompson, 12 February, 1784.

Bradshaw, Robt., Corporal, Contl. Line, 3 years' service.
Du Val, Danl., Captain, Contl. Line, 3 years' service.
Tomlin, Wm., Sergeant, Contl. Line, 3 years' service.
Moore, Peter, Lieut., in Crocketts' Regiment, and served the term.
Wise, Saml., Private, Contl. Line, 3 years' service.
Longwith, Jno., Seaman, State Navy, 3 years' service.
Lunceford, Elias, Sailor, State Navy, 3 years' service.
Wilder, Geo., Sailor, State Navy, 3 years' service.
Reaves, Jas., Sailor, State Navy, 3 years' service.
Sanders, Joseph, Sailor, State Navy, 3 years' service.
Freeman, Hezekiah, Private, State Line, 3 years' service.
Evans, Hy., Private, Contl. Line, 3 years' service.
Isdell, Thomas, Private, State Line, 3 years' service.
Denby, Jonathan, Private, Contl. Line, 3 years' service.
Layne, Josiah, Private, State Line, 3 years' service.
Tompkins, Christopher, Subaltern, Contl. Line, 3 years' service.
Slaughter, Jno., Contl. Line, 3 years' service.
McGuire, Wm. Lieut., Contl. Line, end of war.
Jones, Wm. Sergeant, Contl. Line, 3 years' service.
Wash, Thos., Sergeant, Contl. Line, 3 years' service.
Wash, Benj., Private, Contl. Line, 3 years' service.
Lacy, Hy. R., Private, Contl. Line, 3 years' service.
White, Wm. Capt., Contl. Line, 7 years' service.
Erskine, Chas., Lieut., Contl. Line, 3 years' service.
Self, Larkin, Private, Contl. Line, end of war.
Richeson, Holt, Lieut. Colonel, Contl. Line, 3 years' service.
Penchback, Thos., Sergeant, State Line, 3 years' service.
Jordan, John, Captain, Contl. Line, 7 years' service.
Sneed, John, Private, Contl. Line, 3 years' service.
Cogay, John, Private, State Artillery, 3 years' service.
King, Zach, Private, State Artillery, 3 years' service.
Cawthorn, Wm., Private, State Artillery, 3 years' service.
Bowles, Zach, Private, Contl. Artillery, 3 years' service.
Grabue, John, Lieut., Contl. Line, end of war.
Downey, Michael, Private, State Line, 3 years' service.
Hart, Thos., Private, State Line, 3 years' service.

Broadus, Jas., Ensign, Contl. Line, 3 years' service.

Roe, Wm., Private, Contl. Line, 3 years' service.

Long, Evans, Private, Contl. Line, 3 years' service (orig. voucher says Sergeant for 3 years).

Long, Nicholas, Private, Contl. Line, 3 years' service (orig. voucher says Sergeant for 3 years).

Wolf, Geo., Private, Contl. Line, 3 years' service.

ORANGE COUNTY MARRIAGE BONDS.

(Continued from Vol. IX.)

June 10, 1789. Reuben Spaulding and Fanny Jones. Sec. Elijah Jones.

Dec. 22, 1788. James Roach and Betsey Lindsay. Sec. Caleb Lindsay.

Feb. 28, 1788. Francis Robinson and Mary Terrill. Sec. John Morton.

Mar. 24, 1788. William Robinson and Frankey Adams. Sec. James Adams.

May 26, 1788. John Shelton and Ann Cox. Sec. Thomas Cox.

Feb. 9, 1788. Francis Taylor and Elizabeth Thompson. Sec. William Thompson.

June 30, 1788. John Sanford and Betsy, daughter of William Randell.

Mar. 2, 1789. Reuben Sanford and Frances Webb.

Feb. 6, 1789. John Shadwick and Elizabeth Sanders.

Dec. 26, 1789. Kennuh Sutherland and Ruth Webster. Sec. Dan L. Webster.

Jan. 30, 1789. James Taylor and Sary Hunt.

Jan. 5, 1789. William Taylor and Elizabeth Walker. Sec. Zachariah Taylor.

July 28, 1788. Oliver Terrill and Susannah Mallory. Sec. Wm. Mallory.

Aug. 10, 1789. Andrew Webster and Ursilla Smither.

Oct. 12, 1789. Jesse Watson and Milly, daughter of Phillip Ballard.

Sept. 25, 1789. Jesse Webb and Judah Jones. Sec. Thomas Jones.

Jan. 7, 1788. John Wright and Susan, daughter of Anne Grady.

Feb. 11., 1788. Richard Williams and Nancy Rogers.

Mar. 27, 1788. John Young and Sarah, daughter of Aaron Rogers.

Aug. 11, 1787. Thomas White and Elizabeth Long.

Nov. 26, 1787. William Wright and Rachel, daughter of Perce and Mary Perry.

Jan. 5, 1787. James White and Lucy, daughter of James Wood.

Jan. 31, 1787. Lander Veitch and Peggy Thorpe.

Dec. 24, 1787. Thomas Turner and Catey Brown. Sec. James Brown.

Aug. 1, 1787. Reuben Thomas and Ann, daughter of Joseph Spencer.

July 4, 1787. George Taylor and Ann, daughter of Charity Stanton.

Nov. 7, 1787. Lewis Stowers and Joice, daughter of Elizabeth Shiflett.

Dec. 22, 1787. Edward Spencer and Eleanor Woolfork. Sec. Jos. Woolfork.

Dec. 21, 1787. William Sims, Jr., and Nancy Watts, consent of stepfather, John Douglas.

Dec. 29, 1787. Samuel Self and Frances, daughter of Elizabeth Shiflett.

Sept. 29, 1787. George Scott and Sally Wood.

Mar. 5, 1787. Wisdom Rucker and Rosanna, daughter of Mary Burruss.

Sept. 30, 1787. John Robertson and Frances Porter.

Oct. 22, 1787. George Marshall and Ann Roswell.

Jan. 24, 1787. Fielding Neal and Catherine, daughter of James Beasley.

Feb. 8, 1790. Edward Wright and Frankey Powell.

July	12, 1791.	James Arnold and Eliz. Atkins. Sec. James Atkins.
June	9, 1790.	James Barker and Sarah Maze, widow.
July	31, 1790.	Lawrence Battailed and Ann Hay Taliaferro.
Dec.	6, 1790.	Richard Breeding and Elizabeth Franklyn. Sec. Jonathan Franklyn.
Jan.	8, 1790.	James Brockman and Nancy Bledsoe. Sec. Aaron Bledsoe.
Nov.	17, 1790.	Roger Burras and Cynthia Mills, daughter of Nathaniel.
July	15, 1790.	Abraham Chambers and Mary Dawson, daughter of John.
Feb.	2, 1790.	Thomas Chambers and Milly Robinson.
Aug.	18, 1790.	Jacob Creer and Martha, daughter of Peggy Dollins.
Oct.	19, ——	John Deam and Elizabeth Mays.
Jan.	27, 1790.	Rhodes Dahoney and Jane, daughter of Joseph Chapman.
July	31, 1790.	John Donovan and Sally, daughter of Nathaniel Gaer.
Dec.	6, 1790.	Jonathan Franklyn and Susannah, daughter of Job Breeding.
Dec.	28, 1790.	Benjamin Fortson and Sally, daughter of Job Head.
Aug.	4, 1790.	Richard Howard and Margaret Sullivan.
May	25, 1790.	Nehemiah Hundley and Eliz., daughter of Benj. Cave.
Jan.	30, 1790.	Zach. Lee and Sarah, daughter of Adam and Mary Markspoil.
Dec.	21, 1790.	Thomas Macon and Sarah Madison. Sec. James Madison.
Mar.	15, 1790.	William Mitchell and Rhoda, daughter of Sarah Grinnels.
Dec.	31, 1790.	Gibson Morris and Molly, daughter of Ephraim Knight.
Dec.	27, 1790.	John Owens and Sarah Hambleton, widow.
May	12, 1790.	Robert Paul and Rachel Edwards.

Oct. 27, 1790. William Ramsay and Peggy Barrett.

April 7, 1790. Peter Perry and Lucy Falconer. Sec. Danl. Falconer.

Feb. 15, 1790. James Rumsey and Mary, daughter of Robert Deering.

July 29, 1790. John Simson and Polly Dawson. Sec. John Dawson.

Jan. 28, 1790. John Turner and Sarah Fitzgerald.

June 28, 1790. Benonia Twentyman and Eliz. Natty, widow.

Jan. 25, 1790. Vivian Webb and ———, spinster.

Jan. 15, 1790. Jesse Bennet Webb and Sarah Mason. Sec. Chas. Mason.

Jan. 5, 1790. John Webb and Mildred Lantor. Sec. Jacob Lantor.

Jan. 19, 1790. William Wells and Mary Harvey.

Aug. 24, 1753. Zachariah Warton and Sally Young.

Jan. 9, 1754. Richard Thomas and Mildred Taylor.

Jan. 25, 1754. Moses Lindsay and Mary Donaldson.

April 12, 1756. William Robinson and Joanna Embry.

Jan. 6, 1757. Benjamin Crump, of Round Hill, and Mary Barber Price.

Mar. 21, 1757. Nicholas, son of Robert Green, and Elizabeth, daughter of Agalon Price.

April 5, 1757. George Holland and Mary Coleman.

May 31, 1757. Roland Thomas and Jane Thurston.

Nov. 24, 1757. Rev. Musgrove Dawson and Mary Waugh.

Dec. 21, 1757. John Robinson and Lucy Smith.

Jan. 21, 1758. John Shropshire and Mary Porter.

Jan. 21, 1758. William Robinson and Agnes Smith.

Jan. 27, 1758. Francis Bourne and Fanny Cristofer.

Feb. 10, 1770. William Johnson and Ann Barnett.

Mar. 3, 1770. Moses Stokes and Susan Strother.

Oct. 3, 1770. Bernard Moore and Catherine, daughter of Agalon Price.

May 14, 1771. Reuben Terrill and Mary Walker.

July   8, 1771.   James Gibbs and Mrs. Ann Johnson.

July   20, 1771.   Zachary Taylor and Alice, daughter of Col. Thomas Chew.

July   —, 1771.   Thomas Barbour and Mary Thomas.

Feb.   7, 1772.   John Davis and Mary Jones.

April 27, 1772.   John Willis and Sally Thomas.

May   12, 1772.   John Taliaferro and Ann Stockdell.

May   22, 1772.   Joseph Duncan and Nancy Stevens.

June 23, 1772.   Joel Early and Lucy Smith.

July   26, 1772.   Richard Burnley and Eliza Swan Jones.

Sept. 27, 1772.   Nathan Barksdale and Ann Douglas.

Oct.   29, 1772.   Francis Madison and Susanna, daughter of William Bell.

Nov.   27, 1772.   William Camp and Frances Willis.

April   5, 1773.   Daniel James and Lucy Davis.

June   11, 1773.   Wm. Plumer Thurston and Lucy M. Taliaferro.

Nov.   23, 1773.   Robert Daniel and Frances H. Humphreys.

Oct.   21, 1776.   Andrew Glassell and Elizabeth, daughter of **Erasmus Taylor.**

COLLEGE OF ARMS OF CANADA.

LIST OF SEIGNEURIES AND SEIGNEURS IN ARCHIVES OF COL-
LEGE OF ARMS OF CANADA, LOUISIANA AND ACADIA,
FROM REPORTS OF INTENDANTS, AND PARISH REC-
ORDS, COLLEGE OF ARMS OF CANADA.

(Continued from Vol. IX.)

G.

Gagne-de-Belleavance, Sieur de La Fresnaie (1770).
Gamarche, Sieur de l'Islet (1679).
G. Gardais, Sieur du Pont (1666).
Gazon, Sieur de La Châteignerie (1700).
Giffard, Seigneur de Beauport (1663).
Giffard, Sieur de Targy (1700).
J. Gourdeau, Sieur de Beaulieu (1663).
G. Gourdeau, Sieur de la Grossardière (1700).
Gaston Guay, Sieur de St. François (1670).
J. Guyon, Sieur du Buisson (1663).
Gibien, Sieur de la Baie-des-Chaleurs (1663).
P. Gerbault, Seigneur de Bellegarde (1730).
Gaillard, Sieur de St. Laurent (1690).
Gatineau, Sieur du Plessis (1667).
Gaulties, Sieur de Comporte (1663).
Gaulties, Sieur de Varennes (1667).
Gaulties, Sieur de la Pigeonnière (1700).
J. B. Godefroy, Sieur de Linctot (1663).
L. G. Godefroy de Linctot, Sieur de Normanville (1670).
M. Godefroy de Linctot, Sieur du Fort (1665).
R. Godefroy de Linctot, Seigneur de Tonnancour (1717).
Messire J. B. Godefroy, noble (1663).

Genaple, Sieur de Bellefond (1663).
Genaple, Sieur de Videneuve (1697).

H.

Jacques Hertel, Sieur de Cournoyer (1720).
Jacques Hertel, Sieur de La Fresnière (1700).
Jacques Hertel, Seigneur de Rouville (1720).
F. Herault, Sieur de St. Michel-Gourville (1720).
J. B. Hamard, Sieur de La Borde (1720).
Hamelin, Sieur des Grandines (1720).
A. A. Hamelin, Sieur de La Gannière (1748).
Hébert, Seigneur (1668).

J.

A. Jaret, Seigneur de Beauregard (1676).
Juchereau, Sieur de Maure (1663).
G. Juchereau, Seigneur de La Ferté (1663).
N. Juchereau, Seigneur de St. Denis (1663).
G. Juchereau, Sieur Duchesnay (1685).
Juchereau, Sieur de Beaumarchais (1695).
L. Jolliet, Seigneur d'Anticosti (1672).
P. Jolliet, Chevalier d'Au (1690).
G. Jolliet, Sieur de Mingan (1710).
J. B. Jutrat, Sieur de La Vallée (1715).
J. B. Jutrat, Sieur de La Lusodière (1730).

L.

E. Leborgne, Seigneur de Belleisle (1663).
Leborgne, Sieur de Coudray, (1670).
P. LeBoulanger, Sieur de St. Pierre (1695).
J. Lefebvre, Sieur de la Baie St. Antoine (1675).
Lefebvre, Sieur de Belleisle (1685).
Lefebvre, Sieur Duplessis-Faber (1690).
Lefebvre, Seigneur de Bellefeuille (1750).
Louis LeGou, Chevalier (1695).
LeMarchand, Sieur de Lignery (1695).
Charles LeMoyne, Baron de Longueuil (1700).
LeMoyne, Seigneur de Ste Hélène (1663).

LeMoyne, Sieur de Châteauguay (1663).
LeMoyne, Chevalier de Bienville (1699).
LeMoyne, Sieur de Maricourt (1691).
LeMoyne de Sérigny, Marquis de la Loire (1710).
A. Lafraynay, Sieur de Brucy (1678).
C. de Loreau, Sieur de St. Aubin (1692).
S. Lecompte, Sieur de La Vimaudière (1700).
Lecompte, Seigneur Dupré (1685).
J. Lefournier, Sieur du Vivier (1700).
LeGautier, Sieur de la Vallée-Ranée (1690).
R. LeGardeur, Comte de Tilly (1663).
LeGardeur, Sieur de Repentigny.
LeMoyne, Chevalier d'Iberville (1663).
G. Richard, Sieur de La Fleur (1675).
Rivard, Seigneur de La Vigne (1709).
Rocbert, Sieur de la Morandière (1706).
Rouer, Seigneur de Villeray (1668).
A. Rouer, Sieur de La Cordonniére (1700).
M. Remy, Sieur du Suchet (1725).
Roussel, Sieur de Morambert (1775).
Isaac de Razilli, Comte de Razilli (1632).
J. Razilli, Sieur de l'Isle Bouchard (1663).
C. de Razilli, Sieur de Port Royal (1663).
C. C. Roy de la Poterie, Sieur de Becqueville (1776).

S.

Claude Turgis de St. Etienne, Baron de La Tour (1632).
Charles A. de St. Etienne, Baron de St. Etienne (1660).
Jacques Simard, Sieur de Ramousqué (1750).
Simard, Sieur de la Rivièra du Gouffre (1716).
Simard, Sieur d'Abergemont (1738).
Sacépée, Sieur de Gomicourt (1741).
G. G. C. St. Félix, Chevalier (1767).
Pierre de St. Vincent, Baron de Narcy (1663).
Seigneuret, Sieur de l'Isle (1683).
Pierre de St. Ours, Chevalier (1708).
Soumande, Sieur de Cananville (1663).
Soumande, Sieur de l'Orme (1683).

Sanguinet, Sieur de La Valle (1773).

T.

Jean Talon, Comte d'Orsainville (1685).
Alphonse Tonti, Baron de Paludy (1663).
C. Trottier, Sieur de l'Isle-aux-Hurons (1690).
Trottier, Sieur des Saulniers (1700).

J.

Pierre de Joybert, Comte de Marsan-Coulanges (1684).
F. A. Joannes, Baron de Joannes (1713).
Louis de Joncaire, Sieur de Clairsonne (1759).
Louis de Joncaire, Sieur de Chabert (1710).

K.

N. J. de Kerverzo, nohle (1735).

L.

Louis de Lauzon, Sieur de la Citière (1663).
G. de Lorimier, Sieur des Bardes (1695).
J. du Lignan, Sieur de la Mirante (1684).
Thierry de Lestre, Sieur du Vallon (1663).
Paul de Lusignan, noble (1689).
P. L. de Lusignan, Sieur de Dezmart (1730).

M.

Dominique de La Motte, Sieur de Latier (1676).
Antoine de La Mothe, Sieur de Cardillac (1700).
N. de Marsac, Sieur de l'Homme-Trou (1767).
Etienne de Miray, Sieur de l'Argenterie (1695).
Charles de Montseignat, Seigneur (1700).

N.

Thomas de La Nouguère, Seigneur de la Rivière Ste Anne (1672).
Jacques de Noray, Sieur du Mesnil (1692).
Louis de La Porte, Sieur de Louvigny (1695).
Louis de Niort, Sieur de Noraye (1670).
N. J. de Nozelle, Sieur de Fleurimont (1720).

R.

A. de Rupailly, Sieur des Jardins (1649).
C. de Rupailly, Sieur de Gonneville (1730).
M. de Repentigny, Sieur de Franville (1663).
J. M. de Roy, Sieur de La Barre (1726).
Claude de Ramesay, Comte de la Gesse (1705).
P. P. du Rosy, Sieur de Clarigny (1730).

S.

Jacques de Sabrevois, Seigneur du Bleury (1700).
Pierre de Sorel, Seigneur (1668).

T.

Julien de la Touche, Seigneur de Champlain (1671).
J. A. de Trenel, Sieur de la Pipardière (1694).

V.

J. du Clement du Vault, Sieur de Monceau (1663).
J. de Vasson, noble (1745).
M. de Villebois, Sieur de la Rouvillière (1740).
Louis M. de Vareil, Sieur de Bregonnière (1745).
P. H. C. de Vezin, Sieur de Sionne (1750).
L'Hon. A. Marsolet, Sieur des Prairies-Marsolet (1663).
G. Marsolet, Sieur de Bellechasse (1690).
J. B. Migeon, Seigneur de Bransac (1681).
Migeon, Sieur de La Gauchetière (1700).
J. de Montenon, Sieur de La Rue (1680).
Moreau, Sieur de La Sapino (1680).
Monet, Sieur de Moras (1670).
J. F. Musmache, Sieur de Mingot (1690).
Mangerie, Sieur de La Haye (1663).
Mariachau, Sieur d'Eglis (1710).
Messier, Seigneur de St. Michel (1700).
R. Messier, Sieur du Chêne (1720).
.Messier, Sieur de St. François (1710).
Mouzon, Sieur de La Garde (1765).
P. Melançon, Sieur de La Verdure (1663).
G. P. Maheu, Sieur de la Rivière Maheu (1670).

J. Meleraye, Sieur de La Molerie (1690).
Maray, Sieur de La Chauvignerie (1711).
Marin, Sieur de La Massière (1675).
Marin, Sieur de St. Martin (1750).
Martel, Sieur de La Chesnay (1697).
Martin, Sieur de Lino (1695).
Miville, Sieur de Bonnerencontre (1663).
J. Miville, Sieur des Chesnes (1670.
Morel, Sieur de St. Quentin (1663).
Morel, Seigneur de La Durantaye (1685).
Morel, Chevalier de La Chanalée (1691).
Morel, Sieur du Houssay (1696).
Morel, Sieur de Boisbrillant (1700).
Mariau, Sieur de Pradel (1688).
Mézière, Sieur de Lepervranche (1725).
Morin, Sieur de Beauséjour (1693).
Monmerque, Sieur du Breuil (1730).
A. Mouet, Sieur de Langlade (1785).

N.

Nau, Sieur de Rosambeault (1688).
G. de Noré, Seigneur d'Alençon (1692).
M. Nolant, Sieur de Blainville (1770).
Nouel, Sieur Deljourneau (1735).
Messire Nicolet, Sieur de Bellebonne (1663).
Nepveu, Seigneur de La Noraye (1705).
J. B. Normand, Sieur de Repentigny (1786).

P.

Pajen, Seigneur de Noyan (1665).
M. Pelletier, Sieur de La Prade (1663).
M. Perrot, Sieur de Ste Geneviéve (1670).
J. Perrot, Sieur de St. François-d'Argentenay (1690).
P. Perrot, Sieur de Deryzy (1700).
A. Pécody, Sieur de Contrecoeur (1667).
E. Papin, Sieur de La Ronde (1663).
J. P. Peuvrot, Sieur du Menu (1663).
A. Peuvrot, Sieur de Gardarville (1700).

E. Pezard, Seigneur de La Touche (1665).

P. Picoté, Seigneur d Bellestre (1695).

Piron, Sieur du Long (1663).

J. B. du Portuis, Sieur du Buisson (1675).

M. Poulain, Sieur de La Fontaine (1663).

J. Papineau, Seigneur de Montebello (1789).

LeGardeur, Sieur de Villiers (1663),

LeGardeur, Seigneur d'Alençon (1665).

LeGardeur, Seigneur de St. Pierre (1695).

LeGardeur, Sieur de Beauvais (1695).

LeGardeur, Sieur de l'Isle (1696).

LeGardeur, Sieur de Courtemanche (1700).

LeGardeur, Seigneur de Croisile (1690).

Michel LeNeuf, Sieur du Hérisson (1663).

F. LeNeuf, Sieur de La Poterie (1665).

M. LeNeuf, Sieur de La Vallière (1690).

R. LeNeuf, Seigneur de Beaubassin (1700).

Jean de Lauzon, Marquis de Lauzon (1663).

J. LePellé, Sieur des Marets (1680).

A. LePellé, Sieur de Mézière (1789).

L. Levrard, Sieur de St. Pierre-des-Becquets (1705).

F. Lamoureux, Sieur de Bellevue (1715).

C. Leprohon, Seigneur de La Charité (1715).

G. Legrand, Sieur de Cintré (1760).

P. LeSaulnier, Sieur de St. Michel (1705).

F. Leverrier, Sieur de Rousson (1704).

R. Lepage, Sieur de Rimouski (1700).

D. Lepage, Sieur de St. Barnébé (1720).

Louis Liénard, Comte de Beaujeu (1700).

S. Liénard, Sieur du Bois (1663).

J. Liénard, Sieur de Boisjoly (1695).

G. LeVasseau, Sieur de Néré (1690).

A. Loubia, Sieur de la Rivière Nicolet (1667).

J. Lanouillier, Sieur de Boisclair (1720).

J. B. LeBailly, Sieur de Baillenville (1765).

C. Léringer, Sieur de La Plante (1745).

E. Leseur, Sieur d'Yamaska (1785).

M.

C. de Menou, Comte d'Aulnay-Charnissay (1663).
Philippe de Meuse, Baron d'Entrement (1656).
G. de Meuse, Baron de Pouboncoup (1665).
A. de Meuse, Sieur de Pleinmarais (1700).
Marganne, Sieur de La Valtrie (1680).
Perineau, Sieur de l'Isle-Bizard (1772).
Portail, Sieur de Gevion (1728).
Pothier, Chevalier de Courcy (1717).
J. B. Pothier, Sieur de Ste Gemme (1730).
Pothier, Sieur de La Pommeraye (1730).
Pignet, Sieur de St. Luc (1705).
Poisson, Sieur de Gentilly (1663).
Pollet, Sieur de La Combe (1670).
Prévost, Sieur de St. Thomas (1685).
Péan, Sieur de Livaudière (1724).
Péan, Sieur de St. Michel (1763).
Petit, Sieur d'Yamaska (1695).
Petitpas, Sieur de La Fleur (1663).

R.

René, Robineau, Baron de Portneuf-Bécancourt (1663).
Pierre L. de Rastel, Comte de Rocheblanc (1757).
Philippe de Rigault, Marquis de Vaudreuil (1690).
Riou, Sieur des Trois-Pistoles (1680).
Robutel, Sieur de La Nou (1663).
Robutel, Sieur de Chateauguay (1689).
A. Raineau, Sieur de Granval (1728).
Rainbout, Sieur de Bassalon (1760).
A. Robert, Sieur de La Rochette (1770).
J. Roy, Sieur de St. Lambert (1728).
Roy, Sieur de Montpeine (1735).
J. B. Roy, Sieur de Rimouski (1760).
Ruette, Sieur d'Auteuil (1663).
Ruette, Sieur de Monceaux (1695).
Renaud-Duplessis, Sieur de Dorampont (1690).
M. Renaud-Davenne, Sieur des Mélois (1697).

B. Tessier, Sieur de La Tessonnière (1725).
Testard, Sieur de Montigny (1700).
Tourpin, Sieur du Sault (1670).
Tourpin, Sieur des Ecureuils (1747).
Tremblay, Sieur des Eboulements (1688).
Thiersan, Sieur de Genlis (1730).
Thomas Jacques Taschereau, Seigneur de Ste Marie de La Beauce (1736).

V.

Volant, Sieur de Fosseneuve (1701).

Y.

You, Sieur de La Découverte (1710).

LISTE SUPPLEMENTAIRE.

A.

Mathieu d'Amours, Seigneur de Chaufour (1663).
Louis d'Amours, Seigneur de Gemseg (1690).
Réné d'Amours, Sieur de Clignancourt (1700).
Mathieu d'Amours, Sieur de Fresneuse (1697).
Charles d'Amours, Sieur de Louvières (1698).
Bernard d'Amours, Sieur de Pleine (1700).
Rénére d'Amours, Sieur de Couberon (1736).
Pierre D'Au, Sieur de Jolliet (1700).

B.

Raymond B. des Bergères, Sieur de Rigauville (1694).
Auguste de La Barre, Sieur du Jardin (1714).
François de Bercy, Sieur des Essarts (1724).
Chevalier Louis de La Barthe, Sieur de Livrac.

C.

Louis C. Caderan, Sieur de Bonneville (1687).
Chevalier J. L. de La Corne, Sieur de Chapt (1700).

Jacques du Cailhaut, Sieur de La Tesserie (1663).
J. B. de Coste, Sieur de Mousel de Lantancour (1725).
F. R. de Chanfleur, Seigneur de Villiers (1730).
Hubert de La Croix, Sieur de Maufoie (1732).
N. de Chauvigny, Sieur de Berchereau (1663).
N. de Chauvigny, Seigneur de la Chevrotiere (1686).
J. de Catalogne, Chevalier (1732).
Barthélémy de Courtigny, Sieur de Chandelon (1720).
Louis de La Corne, Sieur de Terrebonne (1740).
Antoine de La Corne, Sieur de la Colombière (1744).

E.

J. de L'Estrignan, Sieur de St. Martin (1670).
Pierre de l'Estaye, Sieur de Peiroux (1720).
Denis d'Estienne, Seigneur de Clerin (1716).

F.

Jacques de Fleury, Seigneur d'Eschambeault (1682).

G.

Messire Perrin Gabar, noble (1670).
Louis de Gannes, Sieur de Falerie (1706).
Georges de Gannes, Sieur de Chamelay (1780).
F. de Galifet, Sieur de Colin (1700).
M. des Goutins, Seigneur de Moscoudabouet (1691).

H.

J. C. de la Houssaye, Sieur d'Etreval (1767).
J. B. C. d'Hastel, Sieur de Rivedoux (1763).

Virginia

County Records

EDITED BY

William Armstrong Crozier, F. R. S., F. G. S. A.

Published by
The Genealogical Association
Hasbrouck Heights
New Jersey

VOLUME X, Parts 2 and 3

1912

IMPORTANT ANNOUNCEMENT

Virginia County Record Publications

EDITED BY

WILLIAM ARMSTRONG CROZIER, F.G.S.A.

With the December, 1912, issue of the "Virginia County Records Quarterly," it will cease to be issued in magazine form, and we shall revert to our initial method of publishing single volumes of the Virginia records. From now on, our books will be privately published and issued to subscribers only.

The new series will consist of 100 copies of each volume, and the price will be $10 net, per volume. Your special attention is called to the small number of copies to be printed, and in order to avoid disappointment, it would be advisable to send in your subscription promptly, as sixty-one subscribers have already been obtained previous to this announcement.

A continued subscription for all forthcoming volumes of the new Series as they appear from the press, will take precedence to the subscription for one volume only, and such single order will be filled only in the event of 100 continued subscribers being unobtainable, an event, however, which we do not anticipate.

The counties covered by the new Series comprise some of the oldest and most important in Virginia. In order to make a connected and complete family history from this section, it has been found from experience that the records in all the counties enumerated below must be examined.

The first book is now on the press, and is devoted to Westmoreland county. The wills and deeds for each county will be brought up to the year 1850. The necessary data for the books mentioned below has already been collected, and it is our intention to publish two to three books each year. Data for other volumes, notably on Northumberland, Stafford, King George and Prince William counties is already being collected and will appear in due course.

It will be well to remember that with the receipt of the 100th subscription, the list of subscribers is positively closed. The volumes will be royal octavo in size, printed in good-sized type on extra heavy paper; indexed, and bound in cloth. Positively no books sent C.O.D. or on approval.

SYNOPSIS OF NEW SERIES OF RECORDS.

WESTMORELAND COUNTY.

Vol. I.   Contents—Abstracts of Wills, etc., 1653—1795.
Land Grants, 1653—1800.
Militia Appointments, 1776—1781.
(On the press. Ready in September.)

ESSEX COUNTY [Including Rappahannock].

Vol. I.   Contents—Abstracts of Wills, etc., 1656—1770.
Land Grants, 1657—1800.
Militia Appointments, 1776—1781.
(Ready in December.)

LANCASTER COUNTY.

Vol. I.   Contents—Abstracts of Wills, etc., 1656—1745.
Land Grants, 1657—1800.
(Ready in April, 1913.)

MIDDLESEX COUNTY.

Vol. I.   Contents—Abstracts of Wills, etc., 1674—1780.
Land Grants, 1672—1800.
(Ready in September, 1913.)

RICHMOND COUNTY.

Vol. I.   Contents—Abstracts of Wills, etc., 1699—1800.
Land Grants, 1692—1800.
Marriage Bonds, 1740—1800.
Militia Appointments, 1776—1788.
Vol. II. Contents—Deeds and Conveyances, 1692—1755.
Vol. III. Contents—Parish Register of Farnham, 1672—1800.
Births, Deaths and Marriages.
(Date of Publication of Vol. I announced later.)

100 *Copies of each Volume—Price,* $10.00 *net.*

THE GENEALOGICAL ASSOCIATION, Publishers
Hasbrouck Heights, New Jersey

CONTENTS

Virginia County Records

AND HERALDIC QUARTERLY REGISTER

Vol. X.	1912	Parts 2 and 3

INDEX TO LAND GRANTS

HENRICO COUNTY.

Book No. 11.

Page.	Name.	Date.	No. Acres.
159	James Holeman	1722	400
159	Matthew Cox	1722	400
199	Charles Evans	1723	788
203	Valentine Ware	1723	262
238	Joseph Mayo	1723	300
238	Same	1723	300
239	John Bowman, Jr.	1723	450
239	John Ealam	1723	140
240	Matthew Ligon	1723	300
240	John Woodall	1723	300
240	Wm. Lewis	1723	400
241	Henry Clay	1723	400
242	Thomas Bott	1723	500
242	Wm. Pride, Jr., and Henry Clay	1723	500
243	Joseph Watson and John Watson	1723	400
243	Joseph Hoopper	1723	200
244	Edward Rivis and Thomas Ally	1723	400
244	Wm. Brown	1723	268
245	George Smith	1723	367½
245	Daniel Hix	1723	275
245	Same	1723	370

246	Ebenezer Adams	1723	400
246	Hutchins Burton	1723	400
247	Thomas Randolph	1723	734
247	Stephen Chastain	1723	219
248	Same	1723	200
292	Thomas Evan	1723	400
302	Thomas Randolph of Henrico County	1723	2,870
303	George Archer of Henrico County	1723	900
305	John James Flournoy	1723	400
307	Rene La Force	1723	1,000
307	Francis Flournoy	1723	400
308	Edward Haskins	1723	300
309	John Welch	1723	400
309	Richard Wade	1723	400
338	James Skelton	1723	1,200
338	Same	1723	400
339	Same	1723	400
339	Same	1723	400
340	John Woodson	1723	400
340	Peter Baze	1723	400
341	Nicholas Cox	1723	400

Book No. 12.

1	Col. Francis Epes	1724	1,000
2	Ebenezer Adams	1724	368
3	Maj. Thos. Randolph	1724	363
3	Constantine Perkins	1724	347A.3R.20po.
4	John Worsham, Jr	1724	400
4	Henry Clay	1724	200
5	Henry Clay	1724	400
5	Same	1724	400
6	John Pride	1724	400
6	Constant Perkins	1724	250
7	Same	1724	250
7	Thomas Neale	1724	350
8	Godfrey Fowler	1724	300
9	Henry Walthall	1724	400

9	James Casson	1724	200
10	John Pattison	1724	350
10	Timothy Harris	1724	350
11	John Lagran	1724	50A.2R.30po.
11	Mark More	1724	400
12	John Hamman	1724	200
13	John Price	1724	390
13	Capt. John Beavill	1724	300
14	William Gording	1724	400
14	Arthur Moseley	1724	400
15	Martha Blankinship	1724	250
15	Thomas Randolph of Henrico County	1724	400
15	Capt. Peter Chastain	1724	377A.1R.10po.
16	Francis Flournoy	1724	400
17	Same	1724	400
18	Same	1724	400
18	Michael Holland	1724	400
19	Same	1724	400
20	Thomas Meridith	1724	400
19	Thomas Farrar	1724	400
20	John Granger	1724	307
21	James Holeman	1724	400
22	Henry Wilson	1724	233
22	James Christian	1724	400
23	George Freeman	1724	320
23	Maj. Wm. Kennon	1724	400
24	Daniel Hill	1724	400
25	John Gill	1724	465
112	John Christian	1724	300
122	Valentine Ware	1724	167
126	Wm. Woodson and Benh. Woodson, Jr.	1724	400
128	John Bolling	1724	343
129	Joseph Scott	1724	400
129	Edward Scott	1724	350
130	Edward Curd	1724	1,200

131	Same	1724	341A.2R.39po.
131	Samuel Burk	1724	400
132	Robert Addams	1724	400
134	Col. Wm. Randolph	1724	4,400
135	John Watson	1724	400
136	Thomas Williamson	1724	200
136	Adam Lavean	1724	262
142	Capt. Richard Randolph	1724	2,700
175	Samuel Hancock and Arthur Moseley, Jr.	1724	500
200	James Nevil	1725	400
209	Henry Chiles	1725	400
230	Tarlton Woodson	1725	300
236	Richard Cocke, Jr., and Benj. Cock.	1725	191
236	Same	1725	374
237	Same	1725	384
237	Same	1725	400
238	Edward Curd	1725	400
238	Same	1725	200
239	Wm. More	1725	300
230	Arthur Moseley, Jr	1725	400
240	John Radford	1725	400
252	Edward Maxey	1725	400
252	Edward Maxey, Jr	1725	400
253	Daniel Worsham	1725	200
253	John Lavillian	1725	400
254	Charles Worsham	1725	300
254	Stephen Beasily	1725	200
282	Thomas Connaway	1725	400
283	Thomas Dawson	1725	400
284	John Price	1725	375
283	John Cannon	1725	50
284	Roger Powel	1725	400
285	Wm. Taylor	1725	200
286	Thomas Farmer	1725	400
287	Wm. Farlowe	1725	137
287	Lewis Tanner	1725	400
288	John Williams	1725	277

289	Henry Hudson	1725	200
289	Henry Clay	1725	330
300	Wm. Bass	1725	350
300	John Dod	1725	281
301	Giles Carter	1725	48
301	Robert Carter	1725	327
302	John Martin, Sr	1725	400
302	Wm. Browne	1725	400
303	Thomas Frankling	1725	200
304	Godfrey Fowler	1725	400
304	Hugh Bragg	1725	135
305	John Russell, Jr	1725	400
305	Wm. Barnett	1725	341
306	Philip Jones	1725	200
307	Charles Clay	1725	150
307	Anne Pride, Jane Pride and Mary Pride	1725	391
308	Robert Hudson and John Ferguson.	1725	400
308	Jonathan Cheatham and Benjamin Cheatham	1725	400
309	John Farmer	1725	400
309	Joseph Irby	1725	400
310	Thomas Frankling	1725	100
310	Robert Willis	1725	350
311	John Andrews	1725	180
312	Wm. Branch	1725	400
312	Wm. Dunifunt	1725	85
313	Wm. May	1725	400
314	Richard Nunnely	1725	350
315	John Pride	1725	328
316	Wm. Locket and Benjamin Locket, Jr.	1725	381
316	Thomas Moss	1725	400
317	George Wilson	1725	350
319	Henry Baugh	1725	250
318	Francis Man	1725	386
320	Henry Vadin	1725	100
320	Robert Willis	1725	400

50   VIRGINIA COUNTY RECORDS.

321	John Pride	1725	247
321	John Lavillian	1725	400
322	Edward Euds	1725	300
323	Francis Worsham and Thomas Tanner	1725	300
323	Lovis Contesse	1725	400
324	Same	1725	400
324	John Worley	1725	277
328	Maj. Thos. Randolph	1725	2,600
329	Dudley Digges of Gloucester County	1725	5,000
330	Mary Blair	1725	1,600
332	John Stewart	1725	1,600
333	Richard Cocke and Benjamin Cocke	1725	6,000
333	John James Flournoy	1725	1,600
334	Alexander Marshall of Henrico County	1725	2,000
336	Peter Ford	1725	400
336	Same	1725	350
337	Matthew Oge	1725	400
337	Same	1725	400
339	Richard Dean	1725	350
344	John Woodrom	1725	400
365	John Man of Henrico Co	1725	395
366	John Woldridge	1725	400
370	Same	1725	370
371	Robert Man	1725	433
371	Gilbert Gee and John Trent	1725	400
372	John Red	1726	400
373	Maj. John Bolling	1726	4,830
374	John Farguson	1725	165
375	Moses Ferguson	1725	400
391	Henry Anderson of Henrico County	1725	900
392	Henry Vadin	1725	700
393	John Woodson of Henrico County	1725	300
393	John Woodson	1725	400

394	Francis Samson	1725	250
394	Walter Scott	1725	400
395	Peter Rowlet	1725	400
396v	Thomas Sanders	1725	400
396	John Newby	1725	100
397	George Worsham, Jr	1725	400
397	Robert Beaslly	1725	400
398	Edward Maxey	1725	400
398	Martin Martin	1725	358
399	Thomas Bayley	1725	229
399	John Peter Bondurant	1725	400
404	John Sanders	1725	400
404	Same	1725	400
405	Jacob Michaux	1725	350
405	Francis Dupuy	1725	200
406	John Phelps	1725	100
406	Hutchins Burton	1725	400
407	John Utley	1725	400
407	Edward Hatcher	1725	200
408	Wm. Weldy	1725	390
408	Leonard Ballow and Thomas Ballow	1725	384
409	John Utley	1725	400
409	John Walters	1725	400
410	John Ellis	1725	400
410v	Anthony Jevodan	1725	200
411	Andrew Moorman	1725	400
411	Henry Webb	1725	400
411	Andrew Moreman	1725	400
412	John Spears	1725	400
412	Thomas Ballow	1725	370
427	Richard Walthall	1725	400
427	Ralfe Jackson	1725	275

BOOK NO. 13.

9	David Mims	1726	358
9	Same	1726	358
11	Col. Wm. Randolph	1726	964
14	James Skelton	1726	1,600

15	Same	1726	750
14	Same	1726	1,600
18	Field Jefferson	1726	897
31	Thomas Totty	1726	500
44	Col. Wm. Randolph	1726	1,159
73	John Bolling	1726	800
74	Col. Wm. Cole	1726	2,000
77	Bowler Cocke	1726	800
78	John Tabor	1726	400
78	Leonard Ballow	1726	300
79	John Burk	1726	300
79	Robert Addams	1726	400
80	Thomas Tindall	1727	400
81	John Lewis	1727	250
80v	Wm. Hodges	1727	380
81	Daniel Thomas	1727	300
82	George Freeman	1727	350
82	Thomas Ballow and Leonard Ballow	1727	400
83	Robert Addams	1727	400
83	Jonas Lawson	1727	400
84	Wm. Towns	1727	400
85	Michael Holland	1727	400
85	Henry Runnals	1727	328
85	Thomas Ballow and Leonard Ballow	1727	400
86	Michall Holland	1727	400
87	Same	1727	400
87	Same	1727	400
88	Same	1727	125
88	Same	1727	400
89	George Stovall	1727	400
152	Thomas Christian	1727	400
157	Wm. Randolph	1727	6,350
164	Capt. John Martin	1727	6,186
193	Col. Francis Epes	1727	2,350
194	Bowler Cocke	1727	400
196	John Woodson	1727	4,934

201	John Johnson	1727	200
201	Henry Harper	1727	400
202	Francis Epes	1727	300
216	Thomas Massie	1727	1,600
217	Daniel Croom	1727	400
218	George Marchbanks	1727	350
218	Warham Eavely	1727	400
219	Same	1727	400
220	Same	1727	400
220	Same	1727	400
221	Same	1727	400
221	Michael Holland	1727	346
222	John Prier and Thos. Christian	1727	400
223	Thomas Christian	1727	400
223	Peter Gerant	1727	400
223	Samuel Arrington	1727	200
224	Charles Christian	1727	400
225	Joel Chandler	1727	400
225	Henry Chiles	1727	400
226	George Stoval	1727	400
226	Wm. Trayler	1727	1,635
227	Benjamin Johnson	1727	326
228	Thomas Randolph	1727	400
282	John Bacon	1727	1,600
348	Col. Wm. Randolph	1729	900
357	Philip Webver	1728	1,050
362	John Parish	1728	400
364	Wm. Moss	1728	400
381	John Martin	1728	400
383	Wm. Spurlock	1728	325
394	John Owen	1728	400
401	Charles Massie	1729	400
401	Same	1729	400
417	Robert Hughes	1729	400
431	Wm. Blackburne	1728	400
439	Anthony Hoggatt	1728	50
466	Thomas Moss	1728	400
488	Wm. Rowlett	1730	300

488	Same	1730	400
497v	Moses Ferguson	1730	400
501	Benjamin Cheatham	1730	300
506	Samuel Good	1730	400
506	Edward Haskins	1730	400
514	Michael Holland	1730	3,761
515	Henry Walthall	1730	400
517	Samuel Good	1730	1,800

BOOK No. 14.

7	Richard Mosby	1728	400
8	John Wright	1728	333
8	Isaac Hughes	1728	400
152	Alexander Marshall	1731	2,578
186	John Watson	1731	400
190	Same	1731	400
336	Charles Christian	1731	200
336	John Watson	1731	400
337	Francis Rice	1731	276
337	Martin Dunkan	1731	400
338	Edward Osborn	1731	200
338	Ralph Jackson	1731	340
339	John Watson	1731	400
340	John Phelps	1731	800
355	Obediah Smith	1731	400
355	Same	1731	400
356	Thomas Conway	1731	400
363	John Langford	1731	300
369	Warham Easly	1731	400
370	Robert Ashurst	1731	1,200
371	John Ferguson	1731	1,365
372	Robert Hancock	1731	400
375	Thomas Owen	1731	400
376	James Hambleton	1731	18
428	Ann Frith	1732	400
513	Richard Wood	1732	400
514	Joseph Wilkinson	1732	400
534	John Peter Perne	1732	122A.2R.24po.
536	Wm. Britton	1732	300

Book No. 15.

10	Thomas Boatwright	1733	322
28	John Watson	1733	400
36	William Patman	1733	400
46	John Cornet	1732	100
63	John Watkins	1733	50
71	Daniel Abney and Abraham Abney	1733	570
80	Abraham Childers, Jr	1733	750
86	Michael Holland	1733	3,450
140	Henry Stokes	1733	400
150	Field Jefferson	1733	800
167	Robert Cole	1733	400
172	Francis Eppes	1733	5,000
179	Edward Haskins	1733	400
181	Frances Jones	1733	200
184	John Maxe	1733	400
185	Richard Randolph	1733	400
196	Jacob Robinson	1734	390
202	Frances Jones	1734	400
203	Allinson Clark	1734	400
207	Francis Eppes	1734	400
238	Thomas Tanner	1734	400
239	Luke Smith	1734	300
247	John Shepherd	1734	200
253	John Childers	1734	400
255	Isaac Robinson	1734	400
260	Thomas Cheatham	1734	400
265	Wm. Williamson	1734	300
267	Wm. Ford	1734	75
341	Wm. Byrd	1734	100
356	Wm. Mosely	1734	760

Book No. 16.

68	John Bow	1735	400
99	James Cock	1735	88
104	Hutchinson Burton	1735	400

112	Benjamin Clark 1735	400
113	Daniel Fitzpatrick and John Ryall.1735	400
117	John Watson 1735	395
180	Daniel Fitzpatrick 1735	393
256	Samuel Richardson 1735	273
294	Henry Holman 1735	343
312	George Freeman 1735	295
462	Samuel Cobbs 1735	4,000
484	John Gibbs 1735	200

BOOK No. 17.

16	John Belcher 1735	229
27	John Puckett 1735	300
37	Thomas Main 1735	250
47	Wm. Jackson 1735	490
103	Peter Hudson 1736	202
103	James Cocke 1736	378
116	John Gun 1736	717
139	John Wheeler 1736	388
211	Peter Jones and Dorothy, his wife, and Henry Battle and Elizabeth, his wife 1736	1,600
236	Wm. Kennon 1736	433
274	Wm. Robinson 1736	400
378	Thomas Totty 1737	268
462	John Farmer 1737	400
467	Same 1737	297
502	Wm. Adkins 1737	251

BOOK No. 18.

10	Benjamin Chalkley 1738	111
33	Jeffery Robinson 1738	400
35	Robert Elam 1738	400
39	Robert Morris 1738	375
52	Jeffery Robinson 1738	384
58	Thomas Rickman 1738	400
66	John Wilkinson 1738	400
88	Wm. Bass 1738	800

94	Thomas Bass	1738	320
123	Robert Ealam	1738	388
182	Wm. Pride	1738	60
226	Wm. Harding	1739	400
229	Daniel Browne	1739	400
232	John Baugh	1739	172
261	Edward Ende	1739	225
321	Thomas Bethell, Jr.	1739	183
343	Thomas Ally	1739	400
370	Thomas Baugh, Jr.	1739	400
397	Benj. Branch	1739	623
442	Robert Mosely	1739	560
514	Gerald Ellison	1739	274
531	Wm. North	1739	71
538	Benjamin Dixon	1739	250
546	Arthur Moseley, Richard Moseley and Wm. Moseley	1739	900

Book No. 19.

576	Gilbert Ealom	1739	440
577	Peter Gill	1739	180
643	Moses Ferguson	1740	400
645	Peter Gill	1740	378
646	Edward Hill	1740	382
650	John Pride, Jr.	1740	399
655	Richard Wood	1740	396
658	Gilbert Elom	1740	650
696	Wm. Pride	1740	137
1061	James Hill	1741	140
1090	John Shepherd	1741	389
1105	John Rud	1741	312
1127	Robert Farguson	1741	288
1139	Abraham Childers	1741	500

Book No. 20.

33	Thomas Gilson	1741	400
38	Joseph Watson	1741	400
40	Same	1741	400

103	James Cocke	1741	246
106	John Price	1741	400
127	Pleasant Cocke	1741	238
121	Wm. Ellis	1741	54
168	Peter Hudson	1741	289
193	John Bowman	1741	255
230	Wm. Harlow	1741	400
254	Joseph Wilkinson	1742	400
260	Thomas Bates	1742	204
339	John Ford and Thomas Vann	1742	178
360	Henry Clay	1742	400
362	Benjamin Burton	1742	400
365	Edward Goode	1742	400
392	Robert Cobbs	1742	400
396	James Young	1742	317
397	John White, Jr.	1742	317
408	John Williamson	1742	310
414	Nicholas Hopson	1742	285
423	Webster Gill	1742	400
431	Wm. Lewis	1742	400
451	Henry Hatcher	1742	314
453	Robert Ealom	1742	380
467	James Farlow	1742	275
495	John Rud, Jr.	1743	400

Book No. 21.

26	Stephen Gill	1742	900
28	John Williamson	1742	340
47	John Watson	1742	121
63	Edward Good	1742	400
109	Wm. Spragen	1742	273
156	Henry Hudson	1742	358
186	John Burton	1742	400
189	Same	1742	133
422	James Rud	1742	400
424	Michael Gawin	1742	400
426	Thomas Harlow	1742	327
488	Joseph Blankenship	1742	112

466	Wm. Hatcher	1742	1,834
483	John Royall	1742	1,000
486	Charles Featherstone	1742	247
501	Peter Baugh	1742	368½
565	Thomas Richardson	1742	354
601	Wm. Belcher	1743	336

BOOK No. 22.

11	Wm. Sharpe	1743	372
48	John Folks	1743	314
61	Josiah Hatcher	1743	398
67	Daniel Price, Jr	1743	174
70	Wm. Blankenship	1743	400
87	Wm. Parker	1743	390
104	Robert Morris	1743	112
125	Wm. Perdue	1743	240
151	James Vaulton	1743	396
158	Charles Holsworth	1743	338
165	John Farmer	1743	196
175	John Williams	1744	360
61	John Price	1744	196
223	Edmond Allen	1744	400
230	Same	1744	400
233	Aaron Haskins	1744	342
303	Hutchens Burton	1745	390
315	Same	1745	191
403	John Nunnaly	1745	246
406	Edward Osborne	1745	400
407	John More	1745	400
413	John Nash	1745	115
459	Jacob Cook	1745	310
462	Wm. Gates	1745	205
463	Abraham Childers	1745	77
540	Wm. Harding	1745	248
541	Jacob Gill	1745	220
542	John Johnson	1745	400
544	Leonard Henley	1745	130
545	John Shoemaker	1745	390

546	Francis Moseley	1745	396
549	Francis Cheetham	1745	383
551	Wm. Williams	1745	256
553	Wm. Mayo	1745	1,060
555	Francis Flournoy	1745	120
556	Same	1745	198
558	Same	1745	1,821
560	Same	1745	181
610	Wm. Pride	1745	20½

Book No. 23.

667	Joshua Irby	1743	366
669	Same	1743	400
700	James Hill	1744	400
702	Joseph Redd	1744	400
760	Thomas Cheatham	1744	224
764	John Hopson	1744	354
777	Thomas Oakley	1744	532
821	Valentine Freeman	1744	400
823	Andrew Leprade	1744	381
827	Thomas Owen	1744	496
829	Wm. Walthall	1744	346
835	Andrew Leprade	1744	103
1025	James Gates	1745	382
1031	Wm. Gates	1745	400
1033	John Roberts and Step. Roberts	1745	298
1037	Samuel Bugg	1745	400
1039	John Bugg	1745	390
1041	David Man	1745	302
1043	Morris Roberts, Step. Roberts, John Roberts and Joshua Roberts	1745	400
1046	Thomas Man	1745	386

Book No. 24.

186	Edward Goode	1745	1,125
377	John Blankenship	1745	227
409	Wm. Chetham	1745	191

Book No. 25.

| 252 | David Man | 1746 | 216 |
| 253 | John Cammel | 1746 | 150 |

Book No. 26.

116	John Wooldridge	1747	314
225	Abraham Baily	1747	450
234	Same	1747	21
236	John Allday	1747	400
453	Peter Hudson	1748	366
550	John Hatchet	1748	390

Book No. 27.

52	Isham Andrews	1748	231
53	Robert Jordan	1748	285
55	John Blankinship	1748	372
58	Richard Dean	1748	224
319	John Labarear	1749	175
387	Thomas Godsey	1749	324
389	Francis Farley	1749	376
391	Wm. Bacon	1749	254
392	James Whitler	1749	404
396	John Farley	1749	17
510	Henry Clay	1749	40
514	Henry Butler	1749	270
516	Samuel Butler	1749	270

Book No. 28.

1	John Skelton	1746	335
2	Same	1746	150
4	Valentine Winfrey	1746	314
5	John Fitzgerald	1746	44½
6	Perrin Giles	1746	156
8	Samuel Jordan	1746	270
9	James Richee	1746	44
238	John Anders	1747	192
239	Benjamin Clarke	1747	90
239	Owen Evan Owen	1747	527
245	Erasmus Oakley	1747	340
305	Randolph Henry	1747	1,790

122	Francis Flournoy 1747	391
565	Henry Hatcher, Jr...............1747	300
596	Nicholas Mealer 1747	300
614	Philip Turpin, Jr...............1747	188

BOOK No. 29.

117	Martin Wilkinson 1750	400
218	Richard Hooper 1750	30
273	Anthony Irby 1750	400
357	Wm. Kennon 1750	630
468	John Walthall 1751	245
469	John Dale 1751	60
471	Cornelius Short 1751	350
473	John Moseby 1751	62
508	Francis Flournoy 1751	120
510	Thomas Connaway 1751	268
519	Richard Norcutt 1751	200
520	Wm. Jenkins 1751	200
522	Same 1751	200
523	Bremillion Hollaway 1751	106
524	Joshua Irby, Jr.................1751	400
525	John Rowlet 1751	27
527	Rowland Blackburn 1751	100
528	John Pride 1751	175
529	George Renyer 1751	42
530	John Condry 1751	380
531	Thomas Moore 1751	158
526	Thomas Womack 1751	164

BOOK No. 30.

134	Richard Belshar 1750	370
149	Michael Jones 1750	92
163	Wm. Warburton 1750	115
454	Alexander Roberson 1750	410
455	Wm. Moore 1750	45
457	Samuel Ligon 1750	179
458	Wm. Burton 1750	410
459	Joseph Bridgewater 1750	179
461	Wm. Bass 1750	463

462	Abraham Salley	1750	30
463	John Walthall	1750	150
465	Gower Dennis	1750	186
466	Same	1750	357
467	Morgan Lester	1750	200

Book No. 31.

438	Michael Jones	1754	186
461	Robert Sharpe	1755	386
508	Stephen Pankey	1755	77
592	Ware Rocket, et als	1755	1,200
593	Wm. Jennings	1755	160
679	John Wilkerson	1755	326
692	Michael Harfield	1755	352
693	Waldgrave Clopton	1755	1,057
193	David Staples	1752	400

Book No. 32.

401	George Wilkerson	1754	200
489	James Hibdon	1754	56
604	Francis George Stegar	1755	2 rds. or 4 lots
605	Same	1755	70
606	Same	1755	12
613	David Whitlock	1755	454
657	John Pleasants	1755	320
679	George Riddell	1756	340

Book No. 33.

242	Thomas Lewis	1756	200
247	Robert Mosby	1756	21
478	John Sheppard	1758	52
597	Wm. Garthwright	1759	102
604	Robert Spears	1759	314
605	Jacob Terress	1759	236
712	John Winn	1760	400

Book No. 34.

42	James Britton	1756	304
61	Joseph Mearitt	1756	100
65	John Williamson	1756	170

140	John Frift	1756	315
176	Thomas Lewis	1757	200
210	Philemon Williams	1757	56
210	Benjamin Bowles	1757	93
211	Henry Ellis	1757	15
243	Benjamin Burton, Jr	1759	198
935	Samuel Duval	1759	46
951	Wm. Smith	1759	276

Book No. 35.

55	Wm. Cocke Radford	1762	76
309	Robert Pleasants	1763	33
444	Abraham Cowly	1763	8
445	Same	1763	6
454	Charles Floyd	1763	19
458	Wm. Adkinson	1763	45

Book No. 36.

608	John Emms	1764	50
776	Thomas Wathins	1765	134
803	Jonathan Williams	1765	129
879	Thomas Goode	1765	273

Book No. 37.

| 382 | Lisby Tipton | 1768 | 8 |

Book No. 38.

487	Richard Randolph	1768	300
528	Joseph Eggleston	1769	250
893	Isaac Younghusband	1770	25
805	Robert Brown	1770	5A.87po.

Book No. 40.

455	Richard Witlock	1771	242
469	David Bowles	1771	234½
679	Robert Pleasants	1772	21½

Book No. 41.

167	Joseph Gathright	1773	245
169	Richard Cottrell	1773	101½
234	Sarah Gottee	1773	5½
296	Julius Allen	1773	One plot or parcel

Book No. 42.

487	Jonathan Williams	1773	24
789	Robert Spiers	1774	286
852	Samuel Duval	1774	100

Book "A."

327	Miles Seldon, Jr.	1780	2

Book "C."

531	Daniel Wade	1781	103

Book "F."

116	Reuben Coutts	1782	45

Book "H."

248	Martin Burton	1783	2
325	Same	1783	4¾

Book "N."

159	James Brittain	1784	100

Book "S."

609	Dabney Miller	1785	44

Book No. 7.

444	Mark Woodcock	1787	127½

Book No. 8.

665	Alexander Young	1787	114

Book No. 10.

575	Thomas Harwood	1787	204
636	Julius Allen	1787	264

Book No. 12.

227	Matthew Clay	1786	140
625	John Allen	1787	193¼

BOOK No. 13.
195 Reuben George 1787   34

BOOK No. 16.
188 John Walker 1788   100

BOOK No. 18.
349 John Price 1788   24½
705 Wm. Reynolds 1788   127

BOOK No. 19.
483 Nathaniel Wilkinson 1789   42½

BOOK No. 20.
13 Wm. Carter 1789   242½
28 Joseph Price 1789   44

BOOK No. 21.
268 Bernard Markham 1789   380

BOOK No. 22.
110 Zenus Tait 1790   13½
111 Charles W. Cottrell 1790   160
389 Daniel L. Hylton...............1790   ½ lot

BOOK No. 23.
55 Hobson Owen, Saml. Williamson,
Joseph Moseby, Hezekiah
Moseby, Wm. Owen, Wm.
Moseby and Nathaniel Wilkin-
son 1790   23¾
461 Joseph Daily 1791   5

BOOK No. 24.
29 Daniel Gordan and Wm. Blades
and Saml. Ege................1791   8
115 Elisha Price 1791   2¼
722 John Mayo 1792   9
723 Same ....1792 48/160 of acre

BOOK No. 25.
59 James Haris 1791   12

NORTHAMPTON COUNTY WILLS

(Continued.)

Bergeron, James, Nuncupative will. 25 Dec., 1727—12 June, 1728. Wife Judith to care for my children and have my estate. Mr. Oliver Hubert Dekrannivett witness to said declaration.

Westcott, John. 16 June, 1728—9 July, 1728. My three children, John Westcott, Elcanah Barker and Frances Ellitt; grandson John, executors; son John and son-in-law Simon Ellitt; witnesses Matt. Floyd, John Satchell, John Esdell.

Briggs, Robert. 24 April, 1728—13 Aug., 1728. Daughters Sarah and Mary; executrix wife Elizabeth; witnesses Jacob Smith, Abram Smith.

Andrews, Andrew. 18 July, 1728—10 Sept., 1728. Sons William, Andrew and John; executrix wife Eleanor; witnesses John Luke, Silvanus Haggoman, Waterfield Dunton.

Core, Rebecca. 7 Feb., 1727-8—8 Oct., 1728. Sons Edward, John and Posthumous; witnesses Arthur Mackallan, Michael Halscutt.

Bowker, Abraham. 1 Sept., 1728—15 Jan., 1728. Wife Mary; to Littleton, son of Edward Belote; to Sarah, daughter of Jerome Griffith; witnesses Elias Roberts, John Yoxon, Gawton Young.

Turner, Edward. 13 Sept., 1728—11 Feb., 1728. Son Edward; daughter Esther Savage; son-in-law Robertson Savage; daughter Sarah Eshon; son George Nicholas Turner; wife Judy; Thomas Savage's daughter Agnes; Nathl. Savage's daughter; to Elishe Belote; executor son George; witnesses Thomas Johnson, Nathl. Savage, Isaac Smith.

White, John. 10 Nov., 1728—11 Feb., 1728. Sons Jacob, John and Caleb; daughters Sarah and Mary; executrix wife Mary; witnesses Luke Johnson, William Vawter, John Tilney.

Nottingham, Richard, Sr. 2 Sept., 1728—13 May, 1729. Son Richard; daughter Johnson Nottingham; sons Joshua, Clark, Jacob and Joseph; daughter Sarah; executrix wife Elizabeth; witnesses John Roberts, Obedience Roberts, Robert Nottingham.

Warren, John, Sr. 20 April, 1729—13 May, 1729. Son Thomas; daughter Sarah; son Moses; brother Hillary; sister Jane Warren; executrix wife Elizabeth; witnesses Joseph Godwin, Mary Warren, William Wilson, John Satchell, John Esdall.

Pole, Godfrey. 17 Dec., 1729—13 Jan., 1729. Grandson William Tazewell; goddaughters Esther and Elizabeth Cable; son George; witnesses Margaret Cable, Anne Hunt, John Freeman.

Hawkins, Gideon, Sr., Planter. 1 April, 1729—10 Feb., 1729. Son John; son Gideon; wife Frances; daughter Sarah; witnesses John Armedying, Thomas Costin, John Hawkins.

Jacob, John. 8 Feb., 1728-9—10 Feb., 1729. Wife Mary; sons William, Thomas and Philip; mentions Abraham Jacob; sons Esau and Isaac; granddaughter Mary Jacob, daughter of John Jacob, Jr.; daughter Elishe; daughter Martha Mapp; executrix wife; witnesses Jonathan Stott, David Bell, Daniel Stott.

Savage, Nathaniel. 15 Dec., 1729—10 Feb., 1729. Son Nathaniel; daughter Ansley; wife Sarah; Mr. Thomas Savage of Cherry-Stones and George Nicholas Turner to be overseers; executrix wife; witnesses Luke Johnson, John Smith, Jonathan Savage, Thomas Savage.

Caple, Hannah. 11 Jan., 1729-30—9 June, 1730. Son Argoll; grandson Stratton Caple; grandson John Burr; granddaughter Esther Burr; grandson Edward Caple; grandson John Caple; grandson Waterson Caple; overseers George Clark and Nathaniel Wilkins; executor grandson Stratton Caple; witnesses Nathl. Wilkins, Robert Trowers, James Ryley.

Pitts, Thomas. 24 April, 1730—9 June, 1730. Son William; son Edmond; executrix wife Elishe; witnesses George Green, Isaac Smith.

Baynton, Robert. 22 April, 1730—9 June, 1730. To William, son of Major William Waters; sister Margaret Waters, widow; friend James Ansele; brother Peter; late father Benjamin Baynton; to Charles Gardner; to Hannah Carter; executor Charles Gardner; witnesses Margaret Force, Thomas Savage.

Roberts, Jacob. 13 May, 1729—9 June, 1730. Brother-in-law Richard Savage; son William Roberts; executrix wife Esther; witnesses William Tankred, Ezekiel Roberts.

Townsend, Jeremiah. 12 April, 1730—9 June, 1730. To Hannah Townsend Halcet; daughter Mary; son Townsend; Letice Halcet, the residue of estate, and she to be executrix; witnesses Andrew Smaw, Gawton Hunt, Anne Hunt.

Kendale, Littleton, Mariner. 5 Jan., 1727—14 July, 1730. Brother William Kendale; mentions his deceased fathers' will dated 3 March, 1719; sister Esther Cable; witnesses Thomas Cable, Mary Cable, Ann Kendale.

Respes, Henry, Planter. 13 May, 1730—10 Nov., 1730. Daughter Lucretia; wife Dorothy; son Richard to be executor; witnesses Peter Bowdoin, William Scott, Henry Speakman.

Smith, Thomas. 22 May, 1728—8 Dec., 1730. Daughter Sarah Custis; daughter Bridget Buntin; daughter Ursley Killam; daughter Mary Nottingham; daughter Tamer Tinley; granddaughter Leah Nottingham; grandson Levin Smith; executor son William Smith; witnesses Thomas Marshall, Posthumous Core.

Roberts, Elizabeth. 27 April, 1731—10 Nov., 1731. Grandson William Roberts; to Littleton Roberts; son Richard Savage; grandson Jacob Roberts; son Edward Robins; son Edward Roberts; my three daughters Esther, Rachel and Elizabeth Roberts; executor son Edward Roberts; witnesses Matt. Harmanson, Jonathan Stott, Isaac Jacob.

Green, Alice. 25 Aug., 1731—14 March, 1731. Son George; daughter Ann Joynes and her daughter Elizabeth; daughter Sarah Floyd; daughter Elizabeth Proctor; daughter Mary Henderson and her daughter Ann Mary; grandsons William and George Green; to Mary Churm; granddaughter Ann Joynes; son Joseph to be executor; witnesses Arnell Addison, Thomas Joynes.

Harmanson, John, Planter. 13 March, 1731-2—9 May, 1732. Wife Isabel; sons John and Kendall; to kinsman John Robins, son of Capt. John Robins; daughters Sarah and Elizabeth; kinsman Peter, son of Major Peter Bowdoin; sister-in-law Bridget Harmanson; executrix wife; friends Thomas Cable, Matt. Harmanson, Henry Harmanson, William Harmanson, Argall Harmanson; witnesses Elishe Stringer, Ezekiel Clegg, Thomas Cable.

Powell, Nicholas. 1 Jan., 1727—9 May, 1732. Sons Abel, William and Benjamin; daughters Sarah, Hannah and Agnes; overseers brother Nathl. Powell and John Stratton; executor son Abel; witnesses John Stratton, Susan Stratton, Ann Johnson.

Sheppard, Joseph. 22 April, 1732—13 June, 1732. To John
son of my brother Jacob; to John Richards; to George
Sheppard, John Lowrey, Elizabeth, widow of William
Batson, Thomas Griffin, Jacob Chapley, Mary Gunderson,
Mary Lunn, William Cowdrey and John Fox; executrix
wife Sarah Sheppard; witnesses John Robins, Jr., John
Sheppard, Mary Gunderson, Andrew Small, William
Satchell.

Sheppard, Sarah. 21 May, 1732—13 June, 1732. Daughter
Rachel Kelly; brother-in-law Kendall Jacob; mentions her
deceased husband, Joseph Sheppard; executor Gawton
Hunt; witnesses Mary Godwin, Anne Hunt, Thomas
Cable.

Stakes, William. 27 April, 1732—11 July, 1732. Wife Rachel;
son Job; all my children; wife to be executrix; witnesses
Thomas Johnson, Obedience Johnson, John Bennet, Spencer Johnson.

Powell, Nathaniel. 12 Aug., 1732—10 Oct., 1732. Sons John,
George and Nicholas; son Joseph; daughter Anne; son
Jonathan; executrix wife Sarah; witnesses Edward
White, Joseph Godwin, Hillary Warren.

Wilson, Thomas. 13 Sept., 1732—12 Dec., 1732. Sons James
and Thomas; daughters Barbary, Ada and Anne; overseers John Webb and Hillary Hunt; executrix wife Abigail; witnesses Hillary Hunt, George Hall, John Webb.

Mapp, Esther. 5 Dec., 1732—13 Feb., 1732. Grandson John
Mapp; granddaughter Sarah Mapp; son Howson Mapp;
to Sarah Kendall; daughter-in-law Leah Mapp; sons John
and Samuel to be executors; witnesses Michael Christian,
Thomas Johnson, Edward Widgeon.

Scott, Henry. 19 Jan., 1731—13 Feb., 1732. Wife Deborah;
sons Joseph, Henry and Daniel; daughter Abigail Barker;
daughter Rachael Parsons; grandson William, son of
Joseph Scott; granddaughter Agnes Pettit, daughter of
John Pettit; daughter Tabitha Linge; executors wife Deborah and son Joseph; witnesses Thomas Marshall, William Tankred, Jonathan Bell.

Harmanson, William. 28 March, 1733—10 April, 1733. Mother Elizabeth Harmanson; sisters Katherine, Esther, Elishe and Elizabeth Harmanson; mother to be executrix; witnesses John Robins, Sr., Andrew Snow, Joseph Toleman.

Preeson, Elizabeth. 8 Sept., 1732—12 June, 1733. Grandson Thomas Preeson; mentions "husband Thomas Preeson;" Grandson John Gibson; son Brown Preeson; daughter Hannah; executors son Brown and daughter Susannah; witnesses Matt. Harmanson, James Hill, Sarah Gibbons.

Cozher, Bartholomew. 28 March, 1733—12 June, 1733. Grandson Thomas Jacob; grandson Josias Jacob; granddaughter Elizabeth Jacob; daughter Naomi Bryant; grandson William Cozher; daughter Ann Heath and son-in-law James Heath; daughter Rahab Scott; grandson Caleb Scott; son-in-law Henry Scott; executrix wife Luranah Cozher; witnesses Arnold Addison, Lurana Johnson.

Freshwater, Elizabeth, no date. 14 Aug., 1733. Sons George, Mark and Mathew; daughter Elizabeth Rascoe; daughter Rossando Loughby; daughter Sarah Costin and her son Matthew Costin; daughter Comfort Dunton; executors sons Thomas and Mark; witnesses Thomas Moor, Frances Moor.

Teague, Thomas. 18 Nov., 1733—11 Dec., 1733. Sons Daniel and Thomas; daughter Rachael Nottingham; daughter Abigail Stott; son-in-law Joseph Dowty; daughter Tamar Teague; daughter Margaret Teague; executors wife Esther and my son Daniel; witnesses Thomas Marshall, William Giddens, Nathl. Dewman.

Johnson, Luke. 26 Nov., 1733—12 Feb., 1733-4. Daughter Rhodea; my eight children, Josiah, Sarah, Luke, Mary, Ann, Keziah, Obediah and Amos; executrix wife Mary; witnesses Thomas Marshall, Hezekiah Tilney, Richard Jacob.

Jones, John. 28 Jan., 1733—12 Feb., 1733. Daughter Ann Mary Jones; daughter Sarah Jones to be executrix; witnesses Margaret Forse, William Bishop.

Waterson, John. 13 Nov., 1733—22 Nov., 1733. Sons William and Richard; sister Sarah Bullock; daughters Abigail, Sarah, Tamar and Mary; wife Elizabeth executrix; witnesses Ralph Pigott, Marriott Parsons, John Groves.

Lattley, Edward. 8 Jan., 1732—12 March, 1733. Children Patience, Elias, Barnabas, Thomas and Morgan Lattley; wife Garbere to be executrix; witnesses Isaac Jacob, John Robins, Katherine Robins.

Major, John. 1 March, 1733—9 April, 1734. Son William; daughter Rachel Pettit; son John; daughter Amy Parker; granddaughter Sarah Major; grandson Littleton Major; grandson John Parker; grandson Major Pettit; wife Winifred and son William executors; witnesses Sorrowful Margaret Cable, Peggy Kendall, Thomas Cable.

Dewman, Jacob. 5 Nov., 1733—9 April, 1734. Daughters Rosannah and Elizabeth Dewman; wife Bridget to be executrix; witnesses Arnold Addison, Nathaniel Dewman.

Dewey, Jacob. 26 Sept., 1732—14 May, 1734. Daughter Tabitha Parker; grandson Jacob Dewey Parker; daughter Beautifilia; wife Matilda executrix; witnesses Edmund Scarburgh, Andrew Allen, Jeremiah Thorp, Alexander Mackallan.

Henderson, Gilbert. 11 April, 1733—14 May, 1734. Sons John, Jacob and Gilbert; daughter Ann Mary Henderson; my brother John Henderson; daughter Susannah Henderson; wife Mary and son John to be executors; witnesses William Bell, Berry Floyd, Thomas Joyne.

Taylor, William, no date. 11 June, 1734. To John Gill; son John Taylor to be executor; witnesses Michael Christian, James Campbell.

Moor, Matthew. 29 March, 1734—10 Sept., 1734. Sons Thomas, Matthew and Jacob; daughter Ann; wife Comfort to be executrix; witnesses John Pigot, Thomas Costin.

Williams, Joseph. 18 Sept., 1734—8 Oct., 1734. Wife Elizabeth sole executrix; witnesses Joseph Godwin, Esther Godwin.

Carvey, Richard. 5 Feb., 1732—8 Oct., 1734. Daughter Mary Scott; son-in-law Salathiel Harrison; granddaughter Mary Harrison; daughter Margaret Billings; daughter Ursula Bell; grandson Abraham Jacob; daughter Anne Dunton; son-in-law Richard Dunton to be executor; witnesses Jonathan Stott, Jacob Waterfield, Elias Dunton.

Turner, Richard. 7 Nov., 1734—10 Dec., 1734. Sons John, Andrew, Richard, Moses and Abraham; daughters Winifred, Mary and Rachael; son Richard to be executor; witnesses Isaac Smith, Abraham Smith, Richard Jacob.

Robins, John, Jr. 28 Nov., 1734—14 Jan., 1734. Son John; wife Susannah; daughter Sarah; my father John Robins; my brothers Edward Robins and William Burton; William Million; wife and father John Robins executors; witnesses Jacob Batson, Mary Godwin, James Flood.

Pettit, Bartholomew. 19 Nov., 1734—14 Jan., 1734. Sons Bartholomew and Jacob; daughters Vienna, Peggy, Mason, Elishe and Ann Pettit; son Bartholomew executor.

Westerhouse, Thomas. Oct. 4, 1734—11 Jan., 1734. Daughters Sarah and Barbary; daughter Sarah to be executrix and estate to be divided between wife and two daughters; probate made by Mordecai Batson and Sarah, his wife, late Sarah Westerhouse; witnesses John Luke, Daniel Luke.

Forse, James. 9 Jan., 1730—8 April, 1735. Cousin Thomas Willand; to brother John Forse, now in England, all my estate in England; wife Margaret executrix; witnesses Thomas Savage, Esther Savage, Sophia Savage.

Snow, Andrew. 25 March, 1735—10 June, 1735. Wife Elishe executrix; sons John, Andrew, William, Caleb and Henry; witnesses John Elligood, Henry Snow, Edward Poyner.

Warren, James. 24 March, 1734—10 June, 1735. Son John and his wife Margaret; grandson William Warren; son John to be executor; witnesses Robert Warren, Jr., Joseph Warren, Sr., John Stratton.

Willett, Hillary 16 April, 1735—10 June, 1735. Sons William, Hillary and Douglas; wife Frances to be executrix; my father to be overseer; witnesses William Willett, William Griffeth.

Johnson, Samuel. 23 Feb., 1734—10 June, 1735. Wife Josephus Maria to be executrix; daughter Mary; daughter Ann, wife of Joseph Batson; son Benjamin; witnesses Caesar Evans, Samuel Mapp, Hillary Stringer.

Jacob, Clark. 6 Jan., 1734-5—10 June, 1735. Wife Margaret Jacob sole executrix; witnesses Michael Christian, Jonathan Stott, Esau Jacob.

Clark, George. 17 Jan., 1731—12 Aug., 1735. Daughters Margaret, Adah, Ann and Sarah; son George; daughter Margaret to be executrix; witnesses William Mills, Thomas Cowdry, Ralph Pigot.

Luke, Daniel. 17 April, 1735—14 Oct., 1735. Nephew Daniel Luke; niece Susannah Luke; niece Ann Luke; brother John Luke; my wife Lydia; witnesses Peter Bowdoin, John Luke, Jonathan Smith.

Harmanson, George. 18 April, 1734—14 Oct., 1735. Grandson Benjamin, son of Argill and Barbary Harmanson; grandson George Harmanson; daughter Barbary Harmanson; son-in-law Arthue Robins and Margaret, his wife; my three daughters Bridget, Henrietta and Rose Harmanson; daughter Isabel Harmanson; son-in-law Hillary Stringer; granddaughter Sarah, daughter of Isabel Harmanson; Elishe, wife of Hillary Stringer; my youngest daughter Rose Harmanson; witnesses John Downy, Henry Harmanson, William Cook to the will of Colonel George Harmanson.

Widgen, Robert, Sr. 15 Jan., 1735—9 Dec., 1735. Sons Robert, William, Edward, Thomas, Jonas and John; daughters Elishe and Susanna; sons Robert, Thomas and John executors; witnesses Caesar Evans, Robert Nottingham.

Stockley, Thomas. 9 Feb., 1735-6—13 April, 1736. Daughters Vallance and Ellen; my brother Woodman Stockley; sister Esther Warren; grandmother Ellen Moor; my wife; brother Woodman executor; witnesses George Hall, Thomas Hunt, Ellen Moor.

Godwin, Joseph, Planter. 26 Jan., 1735—13 April, 1736. Son Archibald; daughters Scarburgh and Elizabeth; my uncle Daniel Godwin; wife Edith executrix; witnesses Solomon Ashby, Daniel Godwin, Eliz. Godwin.

Kendall, William. 19 April, 1736—11 May, 1736. Wife Henrietta; son Littleton; to my mother my part of the estate of my sister Peggy Kendall, deceased; brother George Kendall; Col. Thomas Cable and my wife executors; witnesses Robert Nottingham, Hillary Stringer, John Marshall.

Brickhouse, Jedidiah. 30 March, 1736—11 May, 1736. Son Abner; wife Rachel executrix; witnesses Peter Brickhouse, Major Brickhouse, William Tankred.

Hyron, Mary. 29 July, 1732—8 June, 1736. Granddaughter Mary Chandly; John Chandly; granddaughter Mary Roberts; granddaughter Sarah Carter; my three sons Charles Roberts, John Roberts and Thomas Carter; son Charles Roberts executor; witnesses John Wilson, Grace Wilson.

Stockly, John. 27 March, 1736—8 June, 1736. Son Jonas; daughters Ann and Sarah; son Francis; wife Bridget executrix; witnesses Luke Webb, Peter Bowdoin.

Foster, William. 29 March, 1736—8 June, 1736. To Liska Knight; to Leah Willis; to Thomas Griffith, Jr.; Charles Thompson; Thomas Hunt; sister Mary Foster; sister Esther Griffith; Thomas Griffith, Sr., executor; witnesses Hillary Hunt, Daniel Benthall, Joseph Benthall.

Addison, John. 7 June, 1736—9 July, 1736. Sons Thomas, Jacob and John; daughter Mary; daughter Rachel Doughty and her husband Peter; wife Martha executrix; witnesses Arthur Mackallan, Thomas Addison, Dyal McGregor.

Stott, Daniel. 7 April, 1736—30 July, 1736. My children; son Daniel and my wife Susanna executors; witnesses Thomas Edmonds, Urley Bell, Jonathan Edmonds.

Isdell, John. 21 June, 1736—13 July, 1736. Daughters Ada, Elishe, Patience and Ann; wife Ann executrix; witnesses Joseph white, Henry Warren.

Nottingham, Clark. 3 June, 1736—12 Oct., 1736. To Matthew Harman; son Abel; daughter Peggy Mathews; daughter Naomi Jacob; grandson Clark Nottingham; my wife Mary and my son Abel executors; witnesses John Water, Philip Jacob, Richard Dunton.

Cleft, John. 18 Nov., 1736—14 Dec., 1736. To Mary Bennett; residue of estate to Abraham Collins and he to be executor; witnesses Caesar Evans, Esther Garritson.

Bell, Hannah. 5 Feb., 1735-6—14 Dec., 1736. My late husband George Bell; my three sons George, Jedediah and Ezekiel to be executors; witnesses William Brickhouse, Abigail Brickhouse, Custis Kendall.

Dodd, Joseph. 22 April, 1736—8 March, 1736-7. Children Katherine, Elizabeth and Joseph Dodd; son Thomas; wife Ann executrix; witnesses Robert Watson, John Stripe, Jr., John Stratton.

Edmunds, David. 7 Dec., 1735—13 Jan., 1735. My wife; sons Elijah, Jonathan, David and Thomas; daughters Anne, Joanna and Sarah; sons Elijah and Jonathan to be executors; witnesses Jonathan Stott, Nehemiah Stott, John Mackallan.

Christian, Michael. 22 Dec., 1735—13 Jan., 1735. Eldest son Michael; son William; daughters Sarah, Elizabeth and Susannah Christian; wife Rose to be executrix; witnesses William Smith, Susannah Smith, Nathaniel Rogers.

Jacob, Isaac. 9 Jan., 1735—10 Feb., 1735. To brother Hancock Jacob all my estate; witnesses Littleton Eyre, Peggy Jacob, William White.

Stott, Jonathan, of Hungars Parish. 14 Jan., 1735—10 Feb., 1735. Wife Joanna to be executrix; sons Abel, Laban and Jonathan; daughter Bridget; brother-in-law Benjamin Dolbe; witnesses Edward White, John Walter, Jacob Waterfield.

Jackson, John. 9 Oct., 1735—9 Feb., 1735. Wife Jean to be executrix; eldest daughter Lydia; daughter Comfort; witnesses Arthur Mackallan,. Lydia Jackson, Rachael Mackallan.

Kendall, Peggy, nuncupative, declared by her 5 Jan., 1735—10 Feb., 1735. Sister Anne Custis; brother George Mason Kendall; sister Henrietta Kendall; sister Elizabeth Cable; sister Esther Cable; to Nanny Nottingham; to Elizabeth Marshall, sister of Thomas Marshall; brother William; to Sorrowful Margaret Cable; father-in-law Thomas Cable; sister Custis Kendall; my mother Sorrowful Margaret Cable; witnesses Elizabeth Marshall, Margaret Cable, Anne Nottingham; committed to writing the 7th day of Jan., 1735, about 12 hours after the decease of the said Peggy Kendall, in the presence of Thomas Cable, Anne Custis, Susannah Hutchins.

Paterson, James. 19 Feb., 1735-6—9 March, 1735. All estate to friend Peter Dowty; witness Daniel Eshon.

Terry, John. 8 March, 1735-6—13 April, 1736. Brother-in-law Thomas Dodd; sister-in-law Katherine Dodd; sister-in-law Elizabeth Dodd; mother Ann Dodd; father-in-law Joseph Dodd to be executor; witnesses Robert Wadsed, Abigail Williams, John Stratton.

Baily, Margaret. 24 March, 1735-6—13 April, 1736. To William and John Pettit; to Elijah and Jonathan Edmunds; to William Pettit, Jr., to Amy Pettit; executor Jonathan Edmunds; witnesses Agnes Pettit, Jonathan Edmunds.

Dolby, Benjamin. 19 Jan., 1735-6—13 April, 1736. Daughter-in-law Joanna Stott and her children Abel, Laban, Bridget and Jonathan Stott; Joanna Stott to be executrix; witnesses Littleton Eyre, Jacob Waterfield, Jonathan Edmunds.

80 VIRGINIA COUNTY RECORDS.

Knight, Dixon, Planter. 22 March, 1736—13 April, 1736.
Wife Martha; daughter Ann; son Dixon; daughter Susanna; daughter Abigail; son Southey; son Jonas; son
John executor; witnesses Hillary Hunt, Charles Thompson, Jonathan Stephens.

Hunt, Azariah. 14 March, 1735—13 April, 1736. Wife Ann
to be executrix; daughters Mary and Elishe; witnesses
William Willet, George Willet, John Nelson.

Firkettle, John. 22 March, 1736-7—12 April, 1737. Sister
Comfort Berry; brother William Firkettle; brother-in-
law Cornelius Berry executor; witnesses Rachel Walter,
Barthl. Pettit.

Mapp, John. Daughters Sarah and Ann; son Samuel; wife
Tamar executrix; witnesses Caesar Evans, Thomas Ta-
tum, Rachael Spratlin.

Fathery, Ann. 7 March, 1736—12 April, 1737. Son William;
granddaughter Susannah Griffith, daughter of William
Griffith; Elizabeth Griffith, daughter of William Griffith;
granddaughter Elizabeth, daughter of Luke Griffith;
daughter Ann, wife of William Griffith; grandson Benjamin Fathery; son John executor; witnesses William
Tazewell, Sophia Tazewell.

Moor, Thomas, Planter. 11 Feb., 1736-7—12 April, 1737.
Sons Levy, Matthew and John; daughters Elizabeth, Lesly
and Esther; wife Frances executrix; witnesses Isaac
Moor, Tilney Dixon, Elizabeth Griffen.

Savage, Thomas. 30 May, 1736—12 April, 1737. John Sav-
age, son to Sophia Costin; to Savage Bloksom; daughter
Sarah; wife Esther executrix; witnesses Hillary Stringer,
Henry Harmanson, Rose Harmanson.

Satchell, William.' 30 April, 1737—10 May, 1737. Daughter
Susanna; children Elizabeth Comfort, Sarah Mears, James
and Henrietta Satchell; wife Susanna executrix; witnesses
Hillary Stringer, Nich. Eyre, Benjamin Dixon.

Jenkins, Thomas. 7 Feb., 1733—10 May, 1737. Son Raby-
shaw Jenkins; daughter Mary; son Richard; wife Anne
executrix; witnesses George Harmanson, John Thomas,
Hillary Stringer, Charles Roberts.

Bloksom, Savage. 24 Feb., 1736—14 June, 1737. Wife Mary
and my father Jacob Stringer executors; witnesses Hillary
Stringer, William Brumfield, Esther Stringer.
Dixon, Michael. 9 Nov., 1736—14 June, 1737. Sons Benjamin, John and Tilney; daughter Susannah; wife Elizabeth executrix; witnesses Thomas Marshall, John Benson, Richard Parramore.
Saunders, Esther 2 Nov., 1734—14 June, 1737. Sons Richard and James; to Michael and John Williams; granddaughter Esther Dolby; brother William Dolby; son Branson Dolby executor; witnesses Edward White, John Williams, Elizabeth Dolby.
Wilson, Thomas. 15 Nov., 1734—14 June, 1737. Daughter
Sarah Benson; daughter Susannah Jones; daughter Rebecca Smith; sons Thomas and Solomon; daughter Leah;
daughter Rachel Wilson; daughter Ansly Wilson; grand-
son George Wilson; my wife Susanna and my son Thomas
executors.
Wilkins, John. 27 June, 1731—14 June, 1737. Grandsons
Jonathan, Henry, John and Nathaniel Wilkins; Thomas
Watts; overseers Peter Bowdoin, William Wilkins, Sr.,
Benjamin Stratton, Jonathan Stott, John Wilkins, Jr.;
grandson Jonathan Wilkins executor; witnesses Peter
Bowdoin, William Bromfield, Hillary Willett.
Sanders, Esther. 6 May, 1737—11 Oct., 1737. Son Branson
Dolby; sons Richard and James Sanders; sister Elizabeth
Dolby; brother Thomas Dolby's two daughters Margaret
and Mary; brother John Dolby's two daughters Tamar
and Bridget; brothers John and Thomas Dolby executors;
witnesses Edward White, Elizabeth Dolby.
Forbes, John. 31 Aug., 1737—11 Oct., 1737. Cousin Thomas
Knight; cousin Forbes Turner; friend Isaac Smith; Peter
Doughty; Jonathan Johnson; Mary Gray, daughter of
Dingley Gray; sister Ann Overton; Forbes Turner, son
of Andrew Turner; Robin Parramore, son of Obedience
Parramore; brother Peter Forbes; Dingley Gray and his
wife Mary to be executors; witnesses John Smith, Golden
Fox, John Pitts.

Clay, John. 4 Sept., 1737—11 Oct., 1737. Brothers Isiah, Leverit, Thomas, Benjamin, Benony and Peter; sister Betty Clay; John Segar; mother Elizabeth Warriner executrix; witnesses John Pigot, John Williams, Thomas Spady.

Clegg, Henry. 23 Sept., 1737—14 Dec., 1737. My seven children; son John; son Clark; wife Ann executrix; witnesses Joseph White, Peter Clegg, Amy Clegg.

Stringer, Jacob. 26 July, 1737—14 Dec., 1737. Wife Elishe; daughters Elishe and Isabel; daughter Betty Harmanson Tilney; daughter Mary Blocksom; son-in-law Hezekiah Tilney; cousin Hillary Stringer; grandson Stringer Tilney; my wife and son-in-law Hezekiah Tilney executors; overseers Capt. William Tazewell, Hillary Stringer and Thomas Cable; witnesses Anne Custis, Margaret Cable, Thomas Cable.

Benson, John. 1 Dec., 1737-8—13 Dec., 1737. Son-in-law Thomas Fiske; brother Jonas Benson; John, son of Samuel Benson; Daniel Watson; wife Sarah executrix; witnesses Thomas Marshall, Patience Marshall, William Dunstun.

Dewman, Nathaniel. 25 April, 1729—10 Jan., 1737. Brother Jacob; my three sisters Elizabeth Giddens and Esther and Margaret Dewman; my loving mother; brother Jacob executor; witnesses Richard Parramore, John Parramore, Thomas Marshall.

Eyre, Neech. 7 Jan., 1737—14 Feb., 1737. To Sarah and Kendall Harmanson by virtue of my marriage with Isabel Harmanson; my uncle Matt. Harmanson; my daughter Ann; cousin Littleton Eyre; my aunt Sophia Tazewell; Rose Harmanson; Hillary Stringer and Alicia, his wife; Bridget Eyre and her son Severn; Arthur Robins, Jr.; Isaac Moor; Frances, wife of Joseph Solomon; father-in-law William Burton, Littleton Eyre and William Tazewell executors; witnesses William Tazewell, Thomas Elliott, Robert Trouer.

Warren, Hillary. 26 Dec., 1737—14 Feb., 1737. Brother Joseph; John Lun; John Lowary; William Shores; wife Gertrude executrix; witnesses John Stringer, Thomas Cowdry.

Dillon, John. 20 Dec., 1737—14 Feb., 1737. Wife Patience and my children; witnesses Wm. Waterson, Marriot Parsons.

Lowry, John, of Savage's Neck. 12 Dec., 1730—14 March, 1737. Sons William and Josiah; grandson Thomas Lunn; grandson John Bird; wife Sarah executrix; witnesses Eliz. Bird, Ann Lunn, Edward Poyner.

Watts, Smith. 1 March, 1737-8—11 April, 1738. Granddaughter Elizabeth Scott; John Groves; brother Richard Cox; daughter Sarah Scott; son-in-law William Scott; witnesses John Stratton, William Scott.

Herritage, William. 20 Jan., 1738—14 Feb., 1738. John Herritage; my children Ann and Thomas; Richard Herritage; Wm. Graves; wife Hannah to be executrix; witnesses Frances Clay, John Pigot.

Flat, Jane. 6 May, 1738—10 May, 1738. Ann Dodd; Thomas and Mary Scott; William Scott, Sr., to have residue of estate and be executor; witnesses Benjamin Scott, Margaret Groves.

Johnson, Obedience, Jr., Planter. 19 April, 1738—13 June, 1738. My father Obedience Johnson to be executor; brother Washbourne Johnson; sister Temperance Hughes; brother Richard Johnson; Sarah Smith; witnesses Mary Bevins, John Perry.

Harmanson, Gertrude, widow. 11 Sept., 1732—9 Jan., 1738. Son Henry; grandson Littleton Eyres; daughter Sophia Tazewell; son-in-law Capt. Matt. Harmanson; son-in-law William Tazewell; son-in-law John Stratton; daughter Esther, deceased; grandchildren William, Littleton, Anne and Gertrude Tazewell; kinsman Neech Eyre; brother-in-law Col. George Harmanson; son Henry Harmanson and William Tazewell to be executors; witnesses John Robins, Elias Roberts, Kath. Robins, Margaret Cable, Thomas Cable.

Johnson, Obedience. 14 Aug., 1738—9 Jan., 1738. Grandson
James Johnson; daughter Temperance Hughes; daughter
Bridget Wainhouse; grandson Edmund Hughes; son Obe-
dience; sons Washburn and Richard Johnson to be execu-
tors; witnesses Ezekiel Ashby, Spencer Johnson, John
Roberts.

Batson, Joseph. 4 Feb., 1737—9 Jan., 1738. My father and
mother to keep my daughter Grace; my son Benjamin to
go to his uncle Benjamin Stratton; brother Jonas executor; my wife Mary and daughter Agnes Batson; witnesses
John Batson, Mary Batson.

Payne, Orlando, ———; Feb. 13, 1738. Friend John Luker
all my estate; witnesses John Luker, William Westerhouse, Daniel Luker.

Berry, John (nuncupative will). 13 March, 1738. Wife Margaret; children William, Elizabeth and Sinor Berry.

Harmanson, Susannah, widow. 15 Nov., 1737—9 May, 1739.
Grandson Kendall Harmanson; grandsons Patrick and
John Harmanson; grandsons John Robins, John Bowdoin;
sons-in-law Peter Bowdoin and Matt. Harmanson;
Thomas Cable; daughter Esther Harmanson; Hillary
Stringer; granddaughters Susannah, Sarah and Adah Har-
manson; grandchildren John, Elizabeth and Mary Bow-
doin; executors Matt. Harmanson and Neech Eyre; wit-
nesses John Harper, Hillary Warren, Hillary Stringer,
Littleton Eyre.

Johnson, Obedience. 28 Sept., 1738—9 May, 1739. Sons
Thomas and John; wife Temperance executrix; witnesses
Thomas Abdel, Wm. Dunston, Obedience White.

Joyne, Edward, Sr., Planter. 4 Feb., 1738—12 June, 1739.
Sons John, William, Edward and Harmanson; daughters
Sarah, Margaret; daughter Ann Mekolms; children Tan-
cred and Smart Joyne; son John and my wife Sarah
executors; witnesses Benj. Floyd, William Jacob, Thomas
Hay.

Preeson, Hannah. 6 Jan., 1734—14 Aug., 1739. Peter Bowdoin and my sister Susanna Bowdoin to be executors; witnesses Jonathan Stott, William Smith.

Abdel, Thomas. 12 July, 1728—9 Oct., 1739. Sons Thomas, John and Hancock; daughter Rosanna Stott; daughter Sophia; daughter Martha Addison; wife Martha and son Thomas executors; witnesses Thomas Marshall.

Freshwater, George. 2 June, 1739—9 Oct., 1739. Daughter Elizabeth Mills; son Mark; grandson John Mills; son John and son-in-law Jacob Mills executors; witnesses Isaac Moor, Hillary Hunt, Francis Moor.

Fairfax, James. 11 Jan., 1739—12 Feb., 1739. Godson Fairfax Smith; wife Elizabeth executrix; witnesses Thomas Marshall, Edward Turner, Thomas Janus.

Andrews, Nathaniel. 31 Dec., 1739—12 Feb., 1739. Brothers Jacob, John and Robert; sister Rachael Gascoigne; brother Jacob executor; witnesses Isaac Smith, John Roberts, Kelly Johnson.

Cox, Richard. 7 Jan., 1739—11 March, 1739. Son-in-law Edward Williams; cousins John Groves, Jr., and William Groves; cousin John Groves, Sr., executor; witnesses William Taylor, John Stratton.

Willet, William. 18 Oct., 1739—11 March, 1739. Daughter Elizabeth Gossigan; grandson Thomas Willet; daughters Leah Gossigan and Ann Hunt; grandchildren Mary, William, Hillary and Douglas Willet; my deceased son Hillary Willet; granddaughters Mary and Elishe Hunt; granddaughters Isabel and Mary Senior; daughter-in-law Frances Gelding; my three sons-in-law Thomas and James Gossigan and Thomas Hunt executors; witnesses Hillary Hunt, Roy Johnson, Daniel Benthall; inventory of estate of Capt. Wm. Willet, 5 April, 1740.

Campbell, Simon. 1 Feb., 1739—8 April, 1740. Brother Nicholas Campbell; son-in-law John Roberts; wife Joanna executrix; witnesses Margaret Cable, Thomas Cable.

Pigot, Ann, widow. 20 Dec., 1739—13 May, 1739. Son Ralph; John, son of my deceased son William Pigot; grandson Ralph; granddaughter Ann, daughter of Ralph Pigot; grandson Galen, son of John Pigot; son Culpeper Pigot;

grandson Elijah Pigot; grandson Culpeper Pigot; granddaughter Ann Harnage; Jacob Harnage; granddaughters Tabitha and Polly Pigot; Vespatian and Edela, children of my son John; son Ralph executor; witnesses John Satchell, Edmund Custis, John Respah.

Batson, John. 23 March, 1739—8 July, 1740. Son Jonas; grandchildren Benjamin and Grace Batson; sons Luke and William; children John and Mary Batson; my wife Ann and son Jonas executors; witnesses Southy Satchell, William Dolby, Eleanor Dolby.

Giddens, William. 27 Feb., 1740—8 July, 1740. Sons Thomas, John, William and Jacob; daughter Hannah Douty; wife Elizabeth executrix; witnesses Thomas Abdell, John Smith, Jonathan Douty.

Robins, John, Sr. 13 Dec., 1739—8 July, 1740. Son Edward; my brother Obedience Robins; wife Katherine; grandson John Robins; brother Littleton Robins; my daughters Margaret Burton and Esther Pugh; granddaughter Sarah Robins; grandson William Waters; granddaughter Margaret Burton; Jonathan Roberts; cousin John Robins estate; my wife and sons Edward Robins and William Burton executors; witnesses George Lynch, John Wheeler, Elizabeth Milling, John Williams, Major Gay, Frank Sampson, John Wilkins Watts, Peggy Sampson.

Robins, Obedience, Gent. 19 May, 1731—14 Oct., 1740. Brother John Robins; brother Littleton, deceased; my deceased father; two daughters of my deceased brother Edward Robins; four daughters of my brother Thomas Robins, deceased; two daughters of my sister Grace Stringer, deceased; four daughters of my sister Elizabeth Harmanson; brother John Robins executor; codicil dated 7 July, 1740, revoking legacies to his deceased brother John Robins; my nephew John, grandson of my deceased brother John Robins; nephew Edward Robins; sister-in-law Katherine Robins executrix; witnesses Wm. Tazewell, Wm. Wilkins, Jr., Sarah Wilkins, John Wilkins, John Williams, Nathl. Wilkins, Benj. Jenkins, Margaret Burton, John Richards.

Deyton, Jonathan, of Smith Town, Long Island, at present in
Va. 24 Jan., 1740—10 Feb., 1740. Wife Rachel and my
children; witnesses Abraham Smith, Tankred Joyne,
Thomas Hay, Nehemiah Batson.

Warren, Henry, Sr., Planter. 29 Dec., 1732—10 March, 1740.
Brothers Matthew, Benjamin and Robert; sister Anne
Isdell; brother John Isdell; sister Mary Wilkins; Elishe,
daughter of John Isdell; Patrick Wilkins; John Lunn;
Ann Justice; brother Matthew executor; witnesses
Thomas Snow, Matt. Harmanson, Thomas Cable.

Smith, Geo. 19 Sept., 1741—13 Oct., 1741. Son Littleton;
wife Margaret; daughter Grace; daughter Sarah; wife
executrix; test Geo. Lynch, Jno. Webb, Chas. Webb.

Tilney, Jno. 14 May, 1737—12 Jan., 1741. Son Jonathan;
son Hezekiah; daughter Susanna Smith; daughter Sarah
Tilney; granddaughter Eliz. Tilney and her deceased
father; son Jonathan executor; test Edwd. Turner, Robin
Johnson, Thos. Knight.

Scott, Wm., Sr. 14 April, 1740—9 March, 1741. Son Wm.,
Jr.; son Benj.; wife Mary; daughter Ann Pettit; son
Thomas; son Zerubabel; daughter Mary; wife executrix;
test Robt. Warren, Francis Stokely, Peter Bowdoin.

Warren, Joseph. 13 Jan., 1741-2—9 March, 1741. Son Solomon; son Peter; daughter Rachel; daughter Mary; my
brother Robt. Warren to be executor; test Abner Coffin,
Robt. Warren, Robt. Banks.

Turner, Geo. Nicholas. 17 Dec., 1741—9 March, 1741. Son
George; son Nicholas; son Madox; daughter Margaret;
daughter Ely; daughter Sarah; son Theophilus; son
Joshua; daughter Henrietta; wife Sarah executrix; test
Andrew Stewart, Arthur Roberts, Hy. Bryant.

Waterfield, Southy. 5 Feb., 1737-8—13 July, 1742. Sister
Betty Waterfield; Frances and Esther Watts; brother Jno.
Waterfield; brother Wm. White; father Jno. Waterfield
executor; test Matt Harmanson, Jacob Westerfield, Danl.
Godwin.

Dolby, Wm. 22 June, 1733—13 July, 1742. Sons Joseph and
Stephen and Waterfield Dolby; wife Eleanor executrix;
test Katherine Dolby, Bridget Garret, Nicholas Williams.

Roberts, Jno. 16 Aug., 1737—12 Oct., 1742. Son Isaac; son
Jno.; son Thomas; grandson Emanuel Roberts; granddaughter Elisha Roberts; granddaughter Sarah, daughter
of Isaac Roberts; granddaughter Mary Bell; son Obedience; daughter Eliz. Fisher; Esther Dolby; son Isaac
executor; test Litt. Eyre, Custis Kendall, Esther Evans.

Powell, Sarah, widow of Nathl. Powell. 3 Nov., 1742—9
Nov., 1742. Sons Jno., Nicholas and Joseph Powell; son
Geo.; daughter Ann; son Jonathan; son Jno. executor;
test Wm. Godwin, Mary Widgeon, Thos. Hay.

Willand, Thos. 5 Jan., 1741-2—11 Jan., 1742. Wife Jane;
friend Matt. Harmanson; friend Esau Jacob; cousin Thos.
Welland in Usculme, Devonshire, England, son of my
brother James Welland; Lias, son of Michael Dunton;
Patrick Harmanson; to Capt. Wm. Tazewell; wife executrix; test Jno. Custis Mathews, Silvanus Haggoman, Matt.
Harmanson, Benj. Holmes.

NOTES ON THE COWHERD AND TWYMAN FAMILIES.

(Contributed)
THE COWHERD FAMILY.

In 1066, when William the Conqueror skimmed the cream
of his country, culled out the most energetic of warmen, gath-
ered around him the nobles and knights of Normandy and all
France, marched into England, killed King Harold and took
possession of England, "he built on the spot where Harold
fell" an abbey in memory of his triumph, which he named
Battle Abbey. It was intended for 140 Benedictine monks. In
this abbey was preserved by the monks a so-called "Roll of
Battle Abbey," believed to be a list of those eminent persons

who accompanied the Conqueror to England. The English historian, Rev. Joseph Hunter, believed this roll was of those only who brought families. Hollinshed and Stow each had copies, but they were not alike. However this may be, in one list, at least, will be found the names De Montague, De Buford, De Lacy, De Colbie, Twimyn and De Co-wert (later Co-ward and finally Coward and Cowherd).

History tells us that when the army of the Conqueror came to England it brought the Norman fashion of naming a rich man from his property and a poor man from his trade. Thus these men got their names from Beaufort Castle, Montecute or Montague Castle. Roger de Colbie (Colby) owned the estate and village of Colbie. William de Cowert owned the village of La Cowert. Take almost any of the first settlers of Virginia and you will find the name spelled in several different ways—Barbor, Barber and finally Barbour. So with Colbie, Colby; Cowert, Coward, Cowhard, Cowherd and even Choward (see "British Family Names and Their Meaning").

Both Burke and Sir Henry St. George, in their "Armory" and "Visitations," give the same arms and crest for the Coward or Cowherd family, as follows: Arms—Azure on a chevron gules 3 martlets or; on a chief of the second, a cannon of the third. Crest—A demigrayhound sable, holding between his paws a stag's head argent, attired or.

Sir Henry St. George, in his "Visitation of West Penard, Somersetshire, England," gives the above arms, crest and pedigree of the family of John Coward. From that family came Jonathan Coward to Virginia. His son, Jonathan, married a Miss Colby and had several children, one of which was James, who changed the spelling to Cowherd. His name as an officer in the War of the Revolution is on record at the War Department, and is spelled both ways. He was a man of large estate in several counties in Virginia. Mr. Crozier, in his "Virginia County Records," Vol. 1, mentions him a number of times in lists of deeds given for various tracts of land sold by him in Spotsylvania county, Va., in 1734; witnesses were his friends, Robert Slaughter and Zachary Taylor. The same writer states that he served three years in the Continental Line. He was vestryman many years of St. Mark's Parish.

James Cowherd, son of Jonathan Cowherd and his wife, Frances Colby, married Elizabeth Lacy and had Jonathan, who married Frances Kirtley, daughter of Francis Kirtley, who was Captain in 1755. They had nine children:

(1) Jonathan, Jr., went to Kentucky.

(2) Francis m. Lucy Scott—Maj. in Revolution.

(3) Reuben m. Fanny Woolfolk and settled in Louisa County, Va. Ancestor of R. B. Cowherd, who m. Roberta Robertson Taylor, great-granddaughter of Chief Justice Marshall and granddaughter of Hon. Wm. Winston, member of U. S. Congress.

(4) Yelverton Peyton died unmarried.

(5) Colby, on Feb. 26, 1798, married Tabitha Twyman, daughter of Wm. Twyman, and his wife, Winefred Cowherd, granddaughter of Geo. Twymann, and his wife, Agatha Buford, great-granddaughter of George Twyman, the emigrant, and his wife, Catherine Montague, gr. daughter of Peter Montague, 2nd and grt. gr. daughter of Peter Montague 1st.

(6) Elizabeth m. Isaac Graves of Orange Co., Va.

(7) Drucilla m. Wm. Twyman, Jr.

(8) Tabitha died unmarried.

(9) Fannie died unmarried.

Colby Cowherd, fifth child of Jonathan and Frances (Kirtley) Cowherd, married on Feb. 26, 1798, Tabitha Twyman and had

(1) William Cowherd; born July 13, 1806; died Feb. 6, 1870.

(2) Elizabeth married Graham.

(3) Ann married John Scott.

William Cowherd, born July 13, 1806, died Feb. 6, 1870, married on Feb. 5, 1826, Sarah Ann Hill, born Oct. 25, 1807, died June 21, 1890, daughter of Capt. Ambrose Powell Hill, born March 13, 1785, died Feb. 26, 1858, m. on Feb. 10, 1807, to Frances Twyman, born April 27, 1789, died Sept. 18, 1820, daughter of Wm. Twyman the 2nd, died 1843, and his wife,

Elizabeth Garnett, daughter of James Garnett, gr. daughter of Wm. Twyman the 1st, born 1727, and his wife, Winefred Cowherd, daughter of James Cowherd and his wife, Elizabeth Lacy, grt. gr. daughter of Geo. Twyman 2nd, and his wife, Agatha Buford, grt. grt. gr. daughter of Geo. Twyman the 1st, and his wife, Catherine Montague, gr. daughter of Peter Montague 2nd, grt. gr. daughter of Peter Montague the 1st. This Frances Twyman was niece of Tabitha Twyman, who m. Colby Cowherd on Feb. 26, 1798.

William Cowherd, b. July 13, 1806, and his wife, Sarah Ann Hill, had

(1) Edwin Festus, b. April 2, 1827, d. July 21, 1903, married Susan L. Freeman.

(2) Colby, M. D., b. May 13, 1828, m. Mary Cowherd.

(3) Cornelia died in infancy.

(4) Frances Ella, Feb. 12, 1838, m. Genl. Jas. G. Field.

(5) Powell Hill, born 1833, died unmarried.

Edwin Festus Cowherd, b. April 2, 1827, m. Tuesday, July 24, 1849, Susan Latham Freeman, b. Oct. 11, 1829, d. April 5, 1880, daughter of Gabriel Freeman and his (second) wife Sarah Harrison, b. July 26, 1754, d. Dec. 16, 1842, daughter of Rev. Thomas Harrison, b. Oct. 2, 1750, d. June 21, 1814, and his wife Sarah, daughter of Capt. Cuthbert Harrison and his wife, Frances Barnes.

Gabriel Freeman, b. 1781, d. April 23, 1852, was son of Thos. Freeman and his wife, Susan Latham, daughter of John Latham, grandson of Christopher Holmes Freeman of Gloucester Co., Va. He m. Dec. 9, 1775, Sarah Harrison.

Colby Cowherd, b. May 13, 1828, m. his cousin Mary, daughter of John Cowherd and his wife, Lucy Daniel, gr. daughter of Maj. Francis Cowherd and his wife, Lucy Scott.

John Cowherd and his wife, Lucy Daniel, the former being a son of Maj. Francis Cowherd of the Revolution, had

(1) Mary, m. Colby, son of William Cowherd and his wife, Sarah Ann, dau. of Capt. A. P. Hill.

(2)   Peyton, m. Miss Henshaw.
(3)   Charles, d. s. p.
(4)   Yelverton, d. s. p.
(5)   Frank, m. Lottie Haris.
(6)   Marcellas, m. Addie Haris.

FREEMAN FAMILY.

(Contributed)

Christopher Holmes Freeman, born in Gloucester Co., Va., married Elizabeth ——— and settled in New Kent Co., Va. Later he moved to Spottsylvania Co. and settled at a place called "Ilwordford" on the Rappahannock River. He named his large estate "Travelers' Rest." He is on record at the War Department in Washington, D. C., as having served in the war of the Revolution. Was he an officer? He had six sisters, one of whom married a Pollard, one a Rogers, one a Clark, one a Mansfield, one a Meriweather and one married John Walker of the Isle of Wight Co., Va., who had a son, Freeman Walker, who married Sarah Lorton Minge, daughter of David Minge of Charles City Co., Va. (they were cousins). Her brother, John Minge, married Sallie Harrison of Berkley. Thomas, the first son of Christopher Holmes Freeman, m. Susan, daughter of John and Frances Latham, granddaughter of John and Susan Latham of Caroline and Spottsylvania Co., Va. Another son married Miss Claiborne and had Claiborne, George and others.

Thomas and Susan (Latham) Freeman had Gabriel, b. 1781, d. April 23, 1852, m. March 7, 1826, Sarah (his 2nd wife); daughter of Rev. Thomas Harrison, b. 1750, and his wife, Sarah Harrison (his cousin), daughter of Cuthbert Harrison, member of Committee of Safety for Gt. Wm. Co., Va., and later Capt. of a company of cavalry (James Close Burgesses, p. 90). Hening mentions Thomas Freeman and Philip Latham as "Gentlemen app't by the General Assembly as trustees for a town to be named Jefferson, in Culpeper Co., Va. They were authorized and empowered to lay off ½ acre lots on 25 acres of land given by Joseph Crows. They are to make rules, settle disputes, etc. They were also trustees, etc., for the town of Stevensburg in the same co., Vols. 1 and 15. Another son, Archie Freeman, m. Miss Welsh and Holmes Freeman, another brother of Thomas, m. Miss Robinson. His son, Col. Edward Freeman, m. Martha Bolling of Petersburg, Va. (the widow of Slaughter).

TWYMAN FAMILY.

George Twyman, the first of the name in Virginia, was a resident of Middlesex County. He was dead in 1703 as the inventory of his estate was filed the 3d of May that year. His wife was Katherine ————. A MSS. pedigree compiled by William the grandson of George Twyman in 1811, states that his grandmother was Katherine Montague of Middlesex. She was in all probability gt. granddau. of Peter Montague. The widow m. 2d 5 Sept. 1705 Philip Warrick by whom she had issue.

Issue of George and Katherine Twyman.

1. George.
2. Mary ——————— m. 9. Feb. 1720 Geo. Bristow of Middlesex.
3. Catherine bap. 19 Apl. 1702; m. 13 Apl. 1727 John Tomson of Middlesex.

George Twyman 2d m. Agatha Buford 16 July 1724, dau. of Thomas Buford. The widow m. 2d John Warwick of Middlesex, 8 Mch. 1735; m. 3d John Lee, George Twyman removed to Spolsylvania Co., and his will dated 17 Mch. 1733 was probated there 2 Apl. 1734. The exors. being Thomas Coward and testators wife Agatha Twyman. Issue.

1. Elizabeth b. 28 June 1725; d. 29 Aug. 1727.
2. William b. 20 May 1727.
3. Catherine b. 13 June 1729; m. ——— Dillard. She d. in her 89th year.
4. George b. 29 Mch. 1731.
5. Mary b. ———; m. William Greenwood.

William Twyman was appointed 7 June 1748, guardian to his brother George, and 5 July 1748 guardian to his two sisters Catherine and Mary.

William Twyman m. Winifred, dau. of James Cowherd and his wife Elizabeth Lacy. William in his later years was a resident of Madison County. He had issue nine children. He was a private in the Culpeper County Militia, March 1756 (Crozier's Va. Col. Militia p. 58).

Of the issue data concerning two, William and Tabetha Montague Twyman is known.

1. William, b. 1754 m. Elizabeth, dau. of James Garnett of Essex Co. (will prob. 15 July 1765). Issue.

Reuben b. 11 Dec. 1776; d. 1 Feb. 1814; had son Joel who m. Margaret Buford and had daughter who m. Sebastin Stone and were the parents of William Joel Stone, U. S. Senator 1903-1913.

Anthony Twyman b. 2 Feb. 1779; d. May 1858.

James Twyman b. 26 Aug. 1781; d. 1849.

Elizabeth Montague b. 17 Aug. 1783; d. 1844; m. 1st 25 Feb. 1800, Col. Alexander Willis; m. 2d Col. Joshua Fry.

Ann Twyman m. ——— and went to Ky.

Frances Twyman b. 27 Apl. 1789; d. 18 Sep. 1820; m. 10 Feb. 1807 Capt. Ambrose Powell Hill, his 1st wife; his 2d being Lucy Williams; and his 3d Lucy Kennon.

William b. 14 Sep. 1792; d. Feb. 1801.

Travis Jones b. 16 June 1799; d. 1874; m. Sarah, sister of Lucy Williams. He was Col. in C. S. A.

Tabetha Montague Twyman, dau. of William and Winifred (Cowherd) Twyman, m. 26 Feb. 1798, her cousin Colby Cowherd and had issue.

Elizabeth m. ——— Graham.

Ann m. Major John Scott.

William Cowherd m. Sarah Ann Hill dau. of Capt. Ambrose Powell Hill and his first wife Frances Twyman. They had issue six children, viz.:

Edwin F. b. Apl. 1827; d. 5 June 1903; m. Susan Latham Freeman.

Colby m. Mary Jane dau. of John Cowherd and his wife Lucy Daniel, granddau. of Major Francis Cowherd and his wife Lucy Scott.

Ella Frances m. General James G. Field, Atty. General of Virginia.

Powell, d. s. p.

Cornelia, d. in infancy.

George Twyman, b. 1731, youngest son of George and Agatha (Buford) Twyman; m. Mary Walker, b. 15 Jan. 1734 and had issue Samuel who m. Fanny Rogers dau. of John and Ann Iverson (Lewis) Rogers, granddau. of Mary dau. of Col. William Byrd, 1st of Westover.

www.ingramcontent.com/pod-product-compliance
Lightning Source LLC
Chambersburg PA
CBHW070929270326
41927CB00011B/2781